The Bar Exam is unquestionably the most important test of your life. The grueling multi-day test is the culmination of your years of law study. Those years might seem like a blur, but the information you learned (especially during 1L year) is now vitally important. Only this test stands between you and a career as a lawyer. In this booklet are outlines for all of the major topics covered on the MBE. These are the same outlines that I used to ace the bar exam (updated of course). They are not meant to supplant a bar review course or any course of study, but merely aid you in learning and remembering the volumes of information you will need to pass the bar exam. Good luck!

This booklet contains outlines for the following subjects:
- Commercial Paper
- Conflict of Laws
- Contracts
- Equity
- Evidence
- Family Law
- Federal Jurisdiction and Procedure
- Secured Transactions
- Suretyship
- Torts
- Trusts
- Wills

Commercial Paper

I. Key Concepts

    A. Note – Instrument where maker promises to pay payee. (Where promise by bank to repay = certificate of deposit)

    B. Draft - Instrument where drawer orders drawee to pay payee. (Where payable on demand and drawn on bank – even without words of negotiability = check)

    C. Indorsement – signature other than maker, drawer, or acceptor

II. Holder v. Maker (HDC Rule) A. Negotiable

instrument
1. Writing
2. Signed by maker (drawer)
3. Unconditional
    a. No express conditions
    b. not subject to any other writing c. limitation of
    funds ok
4. Promise or order
5. To pay a fixed amount (with or without interest) – fixed or variable rate
6. Of money
7. No other unauthorized promise
8. On demand or at definite time
9. To bearer or to order at time of issue (unless check) B. Negotiated
1. Order = proper indorsement plus delivery
2. Bearer – mere delivery alone
3. Last indorsement rule =
    a. Special/Order b. Blank/Bearer
C. Holder in due course
1. For value
    a. executed consideration b. antecedent claim
    c. your (depository) bank HDC – if value given (cash check)
2. In good faith
    a. honesty-in-fact, and
    b. observance of reasonable commercial standards of fair dealing
    (merchants test)
3. Without knowledge or notice of overdueness, dishonor, claim defense, forgery, irregularity, or incompleteness which questions authenticity
4. Non-holders in due course a. bulk

        b. estate

        c. judicial sale

   D. Free from personal defenses and claims, but subject to real defenses

        F. Forgery, fraud in factum

        A. Alteration, adjudicated insanity

        I. Infancy, Illegality

        D. Duress, Discharge in insolvency

        S. Suretyship defenses (if notice of suretsyship), Statute of Limitations

        (3years for drafts, 6 years for notes; unless no demand, then 10 years)

        1. FTC amelioration – Human buys consumer goods or services on credit. No HDC rule

        2. Shelter rule – anyone who takes after HDC, gets rights of HDC, except participant

III. Holder v. Indorser (contract of secondary liability – at time of indorsement) A. Presentment

        B. Dishonor

        C. Notice of Dishonor

(Warranty if without recourse or delivery except no warranty against forgery) IV. Holder v. Drawee (none, unless acceptance (certification))

        A. Liable for consequential damages

        B. Drawer Discharge

V. Drawer v. Drawee (contractual relationship)

        A. (Drawer puts money in drawee (drawee acts as agent for collection), and drawee pays out according to drawer's order) – properly payable rule

        B. Where drawee doesn't pay, but should have, drawee liable to drawer for wrongful dishonor.

        C. where drawee does pay, but shouldn't, drawee is liable to drawer for breach of contract

        Exceptions

        1. Fictious indorsements are effective

        2. Drawer negligent in the drafting

        3. Drawer negligent in the notifying

VI. Bank Recovery (Finality)

        A. Where the bank pays on a forged drawer's signature or other mistake (e.g., insufficient funds), payment is final and no recovery is permitted from the innocent party whom the bank paid

        b. Where the bank pays on a forged indorsemet, payment is not final and the bank can recover from the innocent party whom it paid (breach of warranty of presentment) (Right to enforce title)

Conflict of Laws

I. Recognition of Foreign Judgments
    A. problem areas:
        1. must have been proper jurisdiction in rendering court
        2. any defenses to full faith and credit
        3. effects of recognizing a sister judgment
    B. Full faith and credit requirements
        1. proper jurisdiction in the rendering court
        2. judgment on the merits
        3. judgment must be final
    C. Good Defenses to Full Faith and Credit
        1. judgment is penal (punishes offense against public) Π = state
        2. judgment was procured by extrinsic fraud (bribing judge, etc) D. Bad Defenses to
Full Faith and Credit
        1. tax judgment
        2. judgment is contrary to the recognizing state's public policy
        3. mistakes of law and/or fact were made (issue for rendering court) E. Foreign Country
Judgments
        1. Comity given if recognizing courts due process standards are satisfied both in terms of:
            a. jurisdiction was proper (minimum contacts)
            b. fair procedures were used during earlier litigation
    F. Family Law Judgments
        1. Divorce decrees
            a. jurisdiction was proper –one spouse domiciled in rendering state b. person attacking
            jurisdiction isn't estopped from doing so
                i. subject to personal jurisdiction in earlier proceeding ii. played
                meaningful role in earlier proceeding
                iii. privity with parties in earlier proceeding
                iv. marry or remarry in reliance on earlier proceeding
        2. Ancillary maters: property and custody awards a. jurisdiction was
            proper
                i. For property, jurisdiction proper if p.j was proper over spouse whose
                property rights are at issue
                ii. For custody, jurisdiction is proper in the child's home state
            b. Divisible Divorce Doctrine - judgments are severable

II. Domicile (start discussion with why domicile is being discusses)
    A. Domicile of choice – domicile acquired by one who has domicile capacity
        1. physical presence in place
            i. can be very short time
        2. intent to be domiciled in that place i.. don't confuse
            with motive
        3. if multiple residence, primary is domicile

        4. can only acquire a new domicile by perfecting
        two parts in that place
   B. Domicile by operation of law – domicile assigned to one
lacking capacity
        1. Infants will be assigned the domicile of their
        parents or custodial parent
        2. Mental incompetent assigned domicile of parent,
        if after then choice

III. Choice of Law – (law selected by the forum court using its
      choice of law approach) A. Vested Rights Approach
        1. Characterize substantive area of law involved
        2. State the appropriate vesting rule
        3. State what state "wins" – where the rights vest
        4. State the result
   B. Most Significant Relationship Approach (IL Follows)
        1. Under this approach the court will apply the
law of that state which is most significantly related to the
outcome of the litigation. To determine this, they will look at (i)
the connecting facts and (ii) certain policy principles.
        2. Discuss the connecting facts (where and what)
        3. Discuss the policy principles
        4. state what state "wins" and the result
   C. Governmental Interest Approach
        1. Under this approach the court will apply its own
law as long as it has a legitimate interest in the outcome of the
litigation. If it has no legitimate interest, this is a false conflict
case and it will apply the law of another state.
        2. Discuss whether the forum has a legitimate
        interest in the outcome of the litigation
        3. State what state "wins" and the result
   D. Better Rule Approach: Under this approach the
court looks at a variety of factors to determine what is the
"better rule" of law, and then applies it.
   E. Federal courts/ diversity cases
        1. If the forum is a federal district court sitting
        in diversity jurisdiction, the court will apply the
        conflict rules of state in which it is sitting.
        2. If the case has been transferred from
        another district, the court will apply the
        conflicts rules of the transferor state

IV. Specific Substantive Law Areas
   A. Torts
        1. Vested Rights Approach
a. Place of injury
        2. Most significant relationship
        approach/ most significant facts a.
        place of injury
        b. place of
          conduct

        causing
         injury
    c. place of home state
    (domicile/incorporation/place of business)
    d. Place where the relationship between
    parties is centered
3. Intrafamily tort immunity – most significant
fact is place of common domicile
4. multiple state torts – injury greatest in Π's
domicile

B. Workers' Compensation (there is no choice since there is administrative tribunal case and it will always apply its own workers' compensation statute

    1. worker can recover under more than one act but any prior recoveries will be credited against subsequent ones

    2. worker can recover under the worker's comp and in common law tort if the Δ has not been given by immunity under the act

C. Contracts

    1. Threshold Inquiry – Whether there is a valid choice of law provision –

    if so, it governs (look at reasons to invalidate :)

        a. state selected has no reasonable relationship with the contract b. no true mutual assent

        c. If invalidated, court uses its own choice of law approach

    2. Vested Rights Approach/ vesting rules

        a. Contract formation problems: place of execution

        b. Contract performance problems: place of performance

    3. Most Significant Relationship/ Most Significant Facts a. Place of negotiation

        b. place of execution

        c. places of performance d. place of home

    state

        e. place where subject matter is located

        f. Capacity governed by law of the place of execution

D. Property - both restatements have same rules

    1. Real property rule – situs (covers both inter vivos transactions and inheritance matters

    2. Personal Property

        a. Inter vivos transactions

            i. Situs at the time of the relevant transaction b. Inheritance matters

                    i. domicile of the decedent at time of death

E. Family Law

    1. Marriage – if valid where it is performed, recognized everywhere a. exception: domiciliaries temporarily leave state to avoid prohibitory rule (expresses a strong public policy) state will not recognize marriage

    2. Divorce – no choice of law, forum always applies own law

    3. Legitimacy

        a. children born out of wedlock are illegitimate b. If mother married child presumed legitimate

        c. validity of subsequent acts governed by father's domicile

  V. Defenses to choice of law

A. Foreign law is against forum's public policy – almost never accepted

B. Substance/procedure dichotomy – forum will use choice of law to determine which substantive law to apply. If issue is procedure it will apply its OWN law

1. In issue is whether the (fill in applicable type of law) is substantive or procedural, for if it is procedural the forum will apply its own law.
2. Favorite – statute of limitations (procedural)
    a. Exceptions:
        i. time limit set by contract – contract will govern
        ii. borrowing statutes – forum is directed to apply shorter time limit, either forum's or state where action arose
        iii. statute conditions substantive right (forum applies substantive law of another state after using choice of law)
            - if another state's statute creates a substantive right, apply the entire statute including procedural provision
    b. Modern Trend: statute of limitations are treated as "substantive" matters to a basic choice of law analysis. (apply most significantly related state)

Contracts

1) Is there an agreement?
2) Is there any reason this promise or agreement shouldn't be enforced?
3) Was the contract performed?
4) Is there any excuse for non-performance - Is it acceptable to breach the contract?
5) How do the courts enforce the agreements? What are the legal consequences for breach?
6) When do people who didn't make the contract have the rights or duties under the contract?

Sources of Contract Law

- Article 2 of the UCC – if subject matter of K is sale of goods
- Any other kind of K use C/L

BASIC CONTRACT TERMS CHECKLIST

1) Difference between agreement and contract
   a. Agreement-
      i. Meeting of the minds – mutual assent-
   b. Contract
      i. Offer – a manifestation of commitment
         1. Content of the communication will determine if it is an offer
            a. 1st communication contains – fair, appropriate, reasonable – conclude that there is no offer – not sufficiently certain
            b. 1st communication contains – requirements, all, only, solely – if these are key words for an offer- sufficiently certain – requirements contract - offer to enter into a requirements contract
            c. Advertisements and price quotations are not offers
            d. Offer expires after a reasonable time- lapse of the offer
            e. Revocation of an offer – must be timely and made aware to the offeree

Where offers cannot be revoked – option contracts, firm offers, offer has been relied on, where there is an offer to enter into a unilateral contract and performance has begun

- Option k if 1) additional promise not to cancel offer and 2) there is some payment for that promise
- Differences between option K and firm offer
  o Firm offer only applies to sale of goods – ucc 2-207 – there is no requirement for payment
  o Option rule always applies but requires there have been some payment for the promise not to revoke
- Reliance must be reasonable and foreseeable
- where there is an offer to enter into a unilateral contract and performance has begun

- o an unilateral contract is one that results from an offer that requires performance as the only possible method of acceptance
    - ii. Acceptance – who, how, and when on return communication
        1. Who - only the person to whom the offer was made can accept the offer
        2. How - the terms that control the methods of acceptance determine the validity of acceptance
            a. The offer can control the method of acceptance
            b. Default rule – any reasonable method of acceptance is allowed
        3. When –

HYPO: an offer is made by X to Y to paint X's house. There is no verbal response from Y, but instead Y starts painting the house

- RULES for this Fact Pattern
    - o If it was an offer to enter into a bilateral contract the start of performance is an implied promise it is an acceptance it creates a bilateral contract
    - o If it was an offer to enter into a unilateral contract then the start of performance is not enough for acceptance

MAILBOX RULE

- With all communications between the parties (outside of acceptance) is effective only when it is received
- Only an acceptance is effective when it is sent

Look for fact pattern where the offeror and offeree are not in the same place – this will tell you that the mailbox rule is employed. There is some delay in communications AND there are inconsistent communications .

REJECTION

Counter offer – counter offer kills the acceptance and operates as an offer

Conditional acceptance – watch for if, provided, but, so long as – all of these words signal a conditional acceptance which operates as an indirect rejection

Mirror image rule – response in order to be an acceptance must mirror the terms of the offer exactly

UCC 2-207

- Applies only to the sale of goods
- Answers 2 very different questions
    - o Whether there is a contract
    - o What are the terms of the contract
- Is there a contract when the response to the offer has additional terms

- RULE: in a sale of goods situation the response does not require mirror image additional terms are okay

Reasons not to enforce the agreement

- How did the parties deal with each other
- Looking for duress, undue influence, misrepresentation or non-disclosure
  - Duress – physical typically (if you don't enter into this agreement I'm going to kill your entire family, I will rain down upon you fire and brimstone)
    - Economic duress – the concept of economic duress is a new and evolving concept and there is very little case law supporting economic duress as an excuse
    - One must have made an improper threat to the other
    - Secondly there must be no reasonable alternative
  - Undue influence
  - misrepresentation
2) Bilateral and Unilateral Ks
   a. Bilateral -
   b. Unilateral – k results from an offer that can only be accepted by performance
3) Condition and duty – difference between words of condition and duty
   a. Condition
   b. Duty
4) Delegation and novation
5) Expectation interest and reliance interest
   a. Expectation
   b. Reliance
6) Impossibility v. frustration of purpose
7) Parole evidence v. statute of frauds

Corporations

I. Corporate Formation
    A. Pre-incorporation contracts – promoters and subscribers
        1. promoters are persons acting on behalf of a corp. not yet formed
            a. Corp. becomes liable on promoter's contracts when they accept:
                i. express board resolution
                ii. implied acceptance occurs through knowledge and benefits
            b. promoter remains liable until there has been novation between parties
                i. if corp. never forms promoter only liable on pre-incorp. Contract ii. if corp. accepts contract both promoter and corp. liable
                iii. promoters are fiduciaries so no secret profits
        2. subscribers are persons or entities who make written offers to buy stock from not yet formed corp.
            a. irrevocable for 6 months
    B. Formation requirements – de jure corporate status
        1. Incorporators merely sign and file the articles of incorporation
        2. Articles must include: (APAIN)
            a. **a**uthorized shares (max to be issued)
            b. **p**urpose
                i. general purpose clause is fine
                ii. specific statement of purpose and ultra vires rules – limit the action of a corp.
            c. **a**gent and address of registered office d. **i**ncorporators
            e. **n**ame of corporation – must indicate incorporation
        3. By-laws – need not be included
    C. De Facto Corporation Doctrine – a business failing to achieve de jure corporate status is nonetheless is treated as a corporation
    D. Legal Significance of formation of corporation
        1. corporation is separate legal person
        2. shareholders not generally personally liable for debts of corp
    E. Piercing the corporate veil to avoid fraud or unfairness: A shareholder is not liable for the debts of a corporation. Except:
        1. Alter ego – failure to observe sufficient corporate formalities, or
        2. Undercapitalization – failure to maintain sufficient funds to cover foreseeable liabilities

II. Issuance of stock – when a corporation sells its own stock
    A. Consideration for issuance of stocks
        1. par value – minimum issuance prices
        2. no par means "no minimum issuance price"
        3. treasury stock – previously issued and required, may be sold again
        4. acquiring property with par value stock- any valid consideration is fine as long as good faith
        5. directors are liable for the issuance of stock below par value

B. Preemptive Rights
   1. preemptive right is right of an existing shareholder to maintain percentage of ownership when there is a new issuance of stock for cash
   2. preemptive rights must be expressly granted

III. Directors and Officers
   A. Statutory requirements-directors
      1. corporation must have a board with at least 1 member
      2. shareholders elect directors
      3. shareholders can remove a director wit or without cause
      4. Valid meeting
         a. unless all directors consent in writing to act without a meeting, meeting is required
         b. notice of directors' meeting can be set in bylaws
         c. proxies are not allowed. Also, no voting agreements
         d. quorum – must have a majority of all directors to do business
         e. vote – to pass a resolution, all that is required is majority of present
   B. Liability of directors to their own corporation and shareholders
      1. Directors have a duty to manage the corporation
      2. In managing the corporation, the directors are protected from liability by the Business Judgment Rule.
      3. Directors, however, are fiduciaries who owe the corporation duties of are and loyalty
      4. Duty of care – must act with the care a prudent person would use with regard to her own business
      5. Duty of loyalty – A director may not receive an unfair benefit to the detriment of the corporation, unless there has been disclosure and independent ratification.
         a. self-dealing – unfair benefit to herself in transaction with corporation b. usurping corporate opportunities – taking opportunity corp. could have c. ratification – directors may defend a claim by obtaining independent ratification through:
            i. majority vote of independent directors
            ii. majority vote of a committee of at least 2 independent directors iii. majority vote of shares held by independent shareholders
   C. Indemnification of directors and officers
      1.. Corp can never indemnify a director liable to their own corporation
      2. Corp must always indemnify if director wins a lawsuit against another party
      3. Corp may indemnify if:
         a. liability to 3rd parties or settlement with the corporation
         b. director or officer shows that they acted in good faith for corp's benefit c. determination to indemnify made by:
            i. majority of independent directors ii. committee of at least 2
            iii. majority of shares may approve iv. special legal counsel

IV. Rights of Shareholders
   A. Shareholder derivative suits (question is whether corp could bring the suit itself?)
      1. Requirements for shareholder to bring derivative suit
         a. contemporaneous stock ownership – must own at least one share when claim brought and throughout litigation
         b. shareholder must make demand that corp bring suit and be denied
   B. Voting
      1. Only the record owner of shares on the record date has the right to vote
      2. Shareholder voting by proxies. Proxy is:
         a. writing
         b. signed by record shareholder
         c. directed to secretary of corporation
         d. authorizing another to vote the shares e. valid for only 11 months
      3. shareholders vote at properly and specially noticed meetings (major changes)
      4. Quorum – majority of outstanding shares present, unless otherwise in articles
      5. Vote – if quorum present, approved if majority of votes cast
      6. pooled or Block Voting
         a. Voting trusts – formal and enforceable for ten years i. written trust agreement
            ii. filed with the corporation
            iii. transfer shares to voting trustee
            iv. shareholders get trust certificates; and
            v. shareholders retain all other rights except for voting
            vi. duration – generally ten years unless extended by agreement
         b. Shareholder voting agreements – written agreement, to vote shares by terms of the agreement binding + irrevocable w/o filing, no limit
      7. Cumulative voting for directors
         a. multiply number of shares times number of directors to be elected b. right to cumulative voting must be granted in the articles
   C. Right of shareholder to examine books and records – Any shareholder shall have access
   D. Dividends – declared at Board's discretion unless the corp. is insolvent
      1. Priority of distribution
         a. common stock – (pay equally pay last)
         b. preferred stock
         c. preferred stock participating (paid again)
         d. cumulative (pay for previous years)
   E. Shareholder agreement to eliminate corporate formalities
      1. unanimous shareholder election to eliminate formalities in articles, bylaws, or filed written agreement
      2. reasonable share transfer restriction
      3. corporate veil will not be pierced
   F. Limited Liability Companies
      1. original purpose – limited liability and tax status of partnership
      2. Requirements

a. organizers file articles of organization

b. members = shareholders; managers = directors

c. company generally has limited liability and 2 partnership characteristics i. limited duration – article must specify events of dissolution

ii. limited liquidity – must have limit in transferability

iii. members may retain management power, or members may delegate their power to a team of managers

iv. LLC=limited liability, limited life, limited liquidity&limited tax

V. Fundamental Corporate Changes

   A. Recognized fundamental corporate changes

   1. merger, consolidation, dissolution

   2. Fundamental amendment of the articles; sale of substantially all assets

   B. Procedural Steps

   1. Resolution by board at a valid meeting

   2. notice of special meeting

   3. approval by majority of all shares entitled to vote, and by majority of any voting group which has been or will be adversely affected

   4. possibility of dissenting shareholder right of appraisal

      a. a shareholder who does not vote in favor of a fundamental change has the right to force the corporation to buy her share at fair value

      b. actions by shareholder to perfect the right i. ??

VI. Federal Securities Law Considerations

   A. Anti fraud – section 10(b)

   1. scienter

   2. deception

   3. in connection with the actual purchase or sale of securities

   B. Section 16(b) – Short swing trading profits

   1. Applies to:

      a. big corporations – listed on exchange or at least 500 shareholders b. big shot defendant

      c. buying and selling stock within a 6 month period

   2. All profits from short-swing trading are revocable by the corporation

   C. Sarbanes-Oxley Act

   1. reporting corporations

   2. CEO and CFO must certify that based on the Officer's knowledge reports filed:

      a. do not contain material misrepresentation or omissions b. fairly present the financial position of the company

   3. willfully certifying a false report could bring 5mil fine and 20 yrs

   4. if reports need restatement, may recover officer's profits

   5. corporations may also recover any profits made by officers during "black out"

Equity

Six (6) Remedies available at equity

1. Injunctive Relief – Δ is ordered (enjoined) to do or refrain from doing something (permanently or temporarily)
    A. Temporary Injunctive Relief
        i. irreparable harm – need for relief no because trial will be too late (balance hardships)
        ii. Π's likelihood of success (require bond to reimburse Δ) B.
    Contrast: Temporary Restraining Order
        i. Test identical
        ii. Ex parte proceeding (no notice but good faith effort, no adversarial proceeding)
        iii. 10 day limitation
    C. Permanent Injunctive Relief (**I P**ut **F**ive **B**ucks **D**own)
        i. Inadequate legal remedy alternative – No replevin, ejectment or money damages (too speculative, tort threatened, Δ insolvent, irreparable injury, multiplicity of actions)
        ii. Property right (traditional) /protectable interest (modern) requirement iii. Feasibility of Enforcement (Negative – no enforcement issues or Mandatory – possible issues from supervision or compliance)
        iv. Balancing of Hardships –
            a) must be gross disparity
            b) not if Δ's conduct willful
            c) consider monetary award to Π
            d) consider hardship to public v.
    Defenses
            a) unclean hands – improper conduct <u>related</u> to lawsuit
            b) laches – Π waits so long unreasonable and prejudicial to Δ (consider money damages)
            c) impossibility – Δ cannot carry out terms of injunction
            d) Free Speech (defamation or privacy publication branch – injunction denied)
    D. Acts to bind: (i) parties (ii) ee and agents (iii) others acting "in concert"

Trade Secret Misappropriation
*   Trade Secret
*   Taken (better if by improper conduct)
*   Fiduciary duty?
= Third party and taker can be enjoined

Trademark/Trade Name Infringement
*   Protectable mark
*   Infringement? (likelihood of confusion tests)

2. Specific Performance – Δ is required to perform the contract (Cha-Cha Is My Dance) A. Contract is valid (more certainty and definiteness than money damages)

    B. Contract conditions of Π must be satisfied

    C. Inadequate legal remedy alternative (Sellers of land can get s.p.) (ok even with liquidated damages clause)

    D. Mutuality of remedy – "Court will reject the mutuality argument if it feels secure that the Π can and will perform." Provide for simultaneous performance E. Defenses

        i. Equitable defenses

            a. unclean hands b.
            laches

            c. unconscionability – "smell test" at time of contract ii.

        Contract defenses

            a. mistake

            b. misrepresentation

            c. statute of frauds (look for: oral land contract. If so new rule: If one has rendered (i) valuable part performance, (ii) in reliance in the contract, this will take the case out of the statute of frauds and specific performance will be granted.

Specials areas of specific performance

- Equitable conversion – If, Specifically enforceable land sale contract then property interests of buyer and seller are switched. Occurs between execution and closing.
  - o Death: Specifically enforceable contract executed.
  - o Damage/Destruction
    - ☐ Majority Rule: The risk of loss is on buyer, except if loss from negligence of seller.
    - ☐ Modern Trend: The risk of loss is on he seller, except if at the time of loss the buyer has either legal title or possession.
    - ☐ Whoever has risk of loss should get insurance, can be got through constructive trust.
- Personal services contracts
  - o Personal services contract – generally not specifically enforceable (enforcement problems and involuntary servitude)
  - o Covenant not to compete – must:
    - ☐ protect a legitimate interest (unique services) and
    - ☐ be reasonable in both geographic and durational scope.

3. Recission – the original contract is considered voidable and rescinded (**G**ood **D**og)
    A. Grounds for rescission (7): (1) mistake (2) misrepresentation (3) coercion (4) undue influence (5) lack of capacity (6) failure of consideration (7) illegality (all make contract invalid)
        i. Mutual mistake: material fact = rescission, collateral fact no rescission ii. Unilateral mistake no rescission except if non-mistaken party knew or should have known (modern trend: exception for undue hardship)
        iii. Misrepresentation – Π must show actual reliance
    B. Valid defenses
        i. unclean hands ii. laches
        iii. non-defense – Π's negligence
4. Reformation – contract does not accurately reflect the understanding reached cannot adversely affect subsequent BFP (**V**ery **G**ood **D**og)
    A. Valid contract
    B. Grounds for reformation
        i. mutual mistake = reformation
        ii. unilateral mistake no reformation, except where non-mistaken party knew
        iii. misrepresentation = reformation
    C. Defenses
        i. unclean hands ii. laches
        iii. non-defenses: negligence of Π, statute of frauds, parol evidence rule

5. Constructive Trust (Δ has title) – Imposed on improperly acquired property to which defendant now has title. Δ serves as "trustee" and must return the property to the plaintiff.
    A. No adequate legal remedy (property unique) B. Tracing is allowed
    C. BFP prevails over Π
    D. Π prevails over unsecured creditors
    E. Use if property value has gone up

6. Equitable Lien (Δ has title) – Imposed on improperly acquired property to which the defendant has title. Property subject to an immediate court-directed sale. Monies received go to the Π. If the proceeds of the sale are less than the fair market value of the property when it was taken, a deficiency judgment will issue for the difference and can be used against Δ's other assets.
    A. No adequate legal remedy
    B. Tracing is allowed
    C. BFP prevails over Π
    D. Π prevails over unsecured creditors
    E. Use is property value has gone down
    F. Use if Δ's property cannot be traced solely to Π's property

<u>Evidence</u>

<u>**Rules of Relevance**</u>

<u>**401 -**</u> any evidence that tends to make any element of the case more or less likely is relevant
- Very low threshold – most evidence is relevant

<u>**402 – irrelevant evidence is inadmissible**</u>

<u>**403**</u>   <u>**- cumulative evidence, confusion, or more prejudicial than probative**</u>
1) evidence may be excluded if its probative value is substantially outweighed by the danger of unfair prejudice – always argue that probative value outweighs any possible prejudice IF any exists
2) confuses the issues
3) or there is needless presentation of cumulative evidence and it wastes time
- <u>**objections under 403 concede relevance**</u>

<u>**Foundational Rules**</u>

<u>**602 – lack of personal knowledge**</u>
- Lack of foundation – person is not established as having the foundation to have personal knowledge

<u>**701 - testimony of lay witnesses**</u>
- Can testify to anything that is rationally based – a <u>**rationally based perception or opinion**</u>
- Speculation – <u>**testament to the mindset of a 3rd party**</u> – what the other person saw, thought, heard, felt, etc.

<u>**Rules Governing Experts**</u>

<u>**702 – qualifications for a person to be an expert**</u>
- Must meet all 4 requirements to lay foundation for expert
  1) an expert by knowledge, skill, experience, training, or education,
  2) testimony based on sufficient facts and data
  3) testimony is product of reliable principles and methods
  4) the witness has applied the principles and methods reliably to the facts of the case

<u>**703 – opinion of experts**</u>
- Experts rely on hearsay via affidavits – all experts use inadmissible evidence to give opinions
- <u>**Expert can give opinion without disclosing underlying facts – testify that they used depositions or affidavits to come to a conclusion but not the facts of the depositions and/or affidavits**</u>

<u>**704 – ultimate issue**</u>
- 704(a) – ultimate issue is not objectionable (i.e. whether or not it was a suicide)
- 704(b) – must be a criminal case – experts can testify to mindset or condition in civil case – but cannot testify knowledge at the time of the crime (i. e. to what a killer was thinking when he was stabbing someone)
- "Invades the purview of the jury"

<u>**705 – disclosure of underlying facts**</u>
- An expert can give their conclusions without testifying as to what facts were used or what the facts were of the inadmissible evidence (i.e. facts of the affidavit or deposition)
- Expert can give their opinion first and then give the facts later – conclusion first

<u>**Cases**</u>

a. **Frye v. United States**

a. **Holding:** scientific evidence presented to the court must be interpreted by the court as "generally accepted" by a meaningful segment of the associated scientific community. This applies to procedures, principles or techniques that may be presented in the proceedings of a court case.

b. **TEST: general acceptance test** is a test to determine the admissibility of scientific evidence in United States Federal courts. It provides that expert opinion based on a scientific technique is admissible only where the technique is generally accepted as reliable in the relevant scientific community.

b. **Daubert v. Merrell Dow Pharmaceuticals**

a. **Holding:** Rule 702 did not incorporate the Frye "general acceptance" test as a basis for assessing the admissibility of scientific expert testimony;

b. **Relevance and reliability:** This requires the trial judge to ensure that the expert's testimony is "relevant to the task at hand" and that it rests "on a reliable foundation". Daubert v. Merrell Dow Pharms., Inc., 509 U.S. 579, 584-587. Concerns about expert testimony cannot be simply referred to the jury as a question of weight. Furthermore, the admissibility of expert testimony is governed by Rule 104(a), not Rule 104(b); thus, the Judge must find it more likely than not that the expert's methods are reliable and reliably applied to the facts at hand.

c. **Scientific knowledge = scientific method/methodology:** A conclusion will qualify as *scientific knowledge* if the proponent can demonstrate that it is the product of sound "scientific methodology"/derived from the scientific method.

d. **Factors relevant:** The Court defined "scientific methodology" as the process of formulating hypotheses and then conducting experiments to prove or falsify the hypothesis, and provided a nondispositive, nonexclusive, "flexible" test for establishing its "validity":

   i. Empirical testing: the theory or technique must be falsifiable, refutable, and testable.
   ii. Subjected to peer-review and publication.
   iii. Known or potential error rate and the existence
   iv. The existence and maintenance of standards and controls concerning its operation.
   v. Degree to which the theory and technique is generally accepted by a relevant scientific community.

e. Rule 702 now includes the additional provisions which state that a witness may only testify if

   i. the testimony is based upon sufficient facts or data
   ii. the testimony is the product of reliable principles and methods, and
   iii. the witness has applied the principles and methods reliably to the facts of the case.

c. **Kumo Tire v. Carmichael**

a. **Holding:** the judge's gatekeeping function identified in *Daubert* applies to all expert testimony, including that which is non-scientific.

b. **Judge is gatekeeper:** Under Rule 702, the task of "gatekeeping", or assuring that scientific expert testimony truly proceeds from "scientific knowledge", rests on the trial judge.

c. **Extends expert testimony from scientific standard to technical or other specialized knowledge standard**

Witness Refresher

612 Writing used to Refresh Memory
- If a witness uses a writing to refresh memory for the purpose of testifying either :
1) While testifying or
2) Before testifying, if the court determines it is necessary in the interest of justice
   - Then an adverse party is entitled to have the writing produced at the hearing, to inspect it, cross-examine the witness and to introduce into evidence the portions of the writing which relate to the testimony of the witness

Hearsay

801– hearsay
Testifying to what other people or 3rd parties have told you
1) **An out of court statement**
2) **Being offered to prove**
3) **the truth of the matter asserted**
- 801(a) – statement is any oral or written assertion or non-verbal conduct of the person
- **801(d) exclusions to hearsay**
  - **801(d)(1) – prior statements by the wittiness**
    - **Cannot simply offer deposition into evidence – can be used to impeach a witness to prove inconsistencies**
  - **801(d)(2) – admission by a party opponent exclusion rule**
    - **Any statements made by party opponents are admissible in court**
      - **P can use D's witnesses'' statements and vice versa but cannot double up your testimony by allowing P's witness discuss what P's other witness testified to**
    - **810(d)(2)(A) – individual in representative capacity – corporations can offer statements of party opponents and they are not hearsay**
    - **801(d)(2)(D) – when named party is corporation statements made by employees may be excluded from hearsay objections when they are speaking about a matter within the scope of their employment**

802 - hearsay is not admissible except as it pertains to these rules
803 – hearsay exceptions
- **803(1) – present sense impression**
  - Time qualifications – perception, presence, immediately thereafter
- **803(2) – excited utterance**
  - Under stress of excitement caused by the stress or condition
- **803(3) – then existing mental, emotional or physical condition**
  - Testimony to feelings of the 3rd party at a particular time that are manifested
    - i.e. you didn't give me this raise and you know in needed the money – feelings are manifested

- **803(4) – statements made for the purpose of medical diagnosis or treatment**
  - Doctor testifying to what a patient complained of in order to receive treatment or diagnosis is not hearsay
- **803(5) – recorded collection**
  - Recorded recollection can be shown to a witness to refresh their memory
    - i.e. showing an expert a paper or book they wrote when they cannot remember specific research
- **803(6) – records of regularly conducted activity –"Business Records Exception"**
  - 5 requirements
    - Must be made at or near the time

- Must be transmitted by a person with knowledge – person testifying must have knowledge of the record's creation
- If it was the regular activity of the business – something commonly done by the business i.e. legal memos in a law firm
- Testified by qualified witness <u>or</u> are the custodian of the document – custodian means the keeper of the document

- **803(8) – public records and reports – <u>"Public Records Exception"</u>**
  - Reports that are made public – public means made by a government agency
    - Sets forth the activities of the officer or the agency (i.e. police procedures)
    - Or made pursuant to a duty of law (laws and regulations, death certificate)
    - 803(8)(c) Beach Aircraft
- **803(9) –vital statistics rule** – records of data of any birth, death or marriage are admissible
- **803(21) – reputation of character**
  - Requires foundational questions – where was this information learned and when and with whom.
  - Widely known beliefs of a community about an individual's reputation

804 – hearsay exceptions for unavailable declarations

Must prove both 804(a) and 804(b) in court
- 804(a) Must show
  - Unavailable as the rule states (death is unavailable, not wanting to testify is not unavailable)
  - Continue not to follow an order that says they have to testify
- 804(b)
  - Former testimony
  - Statement made impending death
  - Testimony against their interest – i.e. testifying to committing a crime
  - Hearsay within hearsay

<u>Character Rules</u>

404 - improper character evidence

- **Evidence that is going to show action and conformity therewith**
  - Because they acted a certain way in the past does not indicate future performance and <u>**inferences of future performance based on past performance are inadmissible**</u>
- **404(b) – <u>"Prior Bad Acts Rule"</u>**
  - Cannot use prior bad acts to show conformity therewith

405 – reputation, opinion or specific conduct

- **405(a) - the reputation of the individual or opinion of the person testifying about the character of who they are testifying about**
- **405(b) – proof may be made by specific instances of the individuals conduct**
  - i.e. if there were case law in which character evidence were admissible, you can offer specific instances and they do not qualify as action in conformity

607 - impeaching a witness

- the credibility of a witness may be attacked by anyone and is always admissible

608 - evidence of character

Can offer evidence of a person's character if it goes to their character of truthfulness

- **608(a) – credibility of witness may be attacked if:**
    - (1) the evidence may refer only to character for truthfulness or untruthfulness, and (2) evidence of truthful character is admissible only after the character of the witness for truthfulness has been attacked by opinion or reputation evidence or otherwise.
- **608(b) – specific instances of conduct may be used to attack character truthfulness**
    - If it is not a crime but simply evidence that they were dishonest or untruthful

609 – impeachment by evidence of conviction of a crime

- **For purpose of attacking character of truthfulness (whether the person is honest) conviction of a crime can be used**
    - if the crime was punishable by death or imprisonment in excess of one year
    - crimes that go to dishonesty
    - crim infalse – crimes of dishonesty, and crimes of dishonesty are always admissible

Family Law

I. Breach of Promise to Marry
  A. History
    1. common law actions
    2. Elements:
      a. contract
      b. breach
      c. damages – (non refundable deposit for ballroom, photographer)
  B. Consideration isn't:
    1. Sex
    2. promises in consideration of marriage
  C. Consideration is a mutual promise
  D. consideration can be oral

II. Marriage
  A. Ceremonial (requires license & solemnization)
    1. Licenses
      a. Medical
        i. purpose – notice the other person
        ii. procedural requirement, not public policy
          o good faith attempt is enough
          o can be waived
      b. Capacity – public policy requirement
        i. sane ii.
        adult
        iii. not related
          o ancestors
          o descendants
          o laterals to first degree iv.
        single
    2. Solemnization
      a. procedural requirement, not public policy; therefore:
        i. good faith is enough
        ii. unauthorized celebrant does not invalidate marriage
  B. Common Law (not in IL)
    1. Capacity SANS?
    2. Words and acts
      a. exchange of consents
      b. cohabitation c.
      holding out
    3. validity: a marriage valid where performed us valid everywhere
  C. Gifts
    1. If conditional
      a. guy gets ring back
    2. If unconditional

  a. girl keeps watch, clock, and mink coat

D. Constitutional privacy

 1. Elements:

  a. Fundamental Right

  b. Test: Compelling justification c. Burden on state

 2. Found in (CAMPER):

  a. Contraception b. Abortion

   i. pre-fetal viability – regulation is okay but cannot be undue burden ii. post-fetal viability – can be prohibited except health of mother

  c. Marriage – race regulations unconstitutional

  d. Procreation – sterilizing criminals unconstitutional e. Education and control of children and parents

  f. Related parties living together – zoning ordinance prohibiting unconstitutional

 3. Not found in (BUSHES): [rights not fundamental, test: rationality, on individual]

  a. Bankruptcy

  b. Unrelated parties living together c. Sodomy

  d. Housing

  e. Education of Self f. Status of Welfare

  III. Termination of Marriage

A. Annulment (judgment of invalidity of marriage) – impediment before marriage

 1. Void – complete nullity – marriage never existed a. no decree necessary

  b. Non waivable defects i. bigamy

   ii. Consanguinity

   iii. insanity

  c. Impediment removed – marriage can go up in status d. 3rd party challenges permissible

 2. Voidable – capable of voiding a. Defects waivable

   i. Fraud going to essentials of marriage

    • yes- religion, pregnancy, normal sex life

    • no - money ii. duress

   iii. intoxication iv. nonage

   v. lack of physical capacity (uncurable impotency)

  b. No 3rd party challenges (only innocent party)

B. Divorce (dissolution of marriage) – impediment after marriage

1. Jurisdiction in rem
    a. Only Π need be a bona fide domiciliary
    b. No money or custody unless personal jurisdiction over Δ
    c. Order is final so full faith and credit under Article VI
2. No-fault (irretrievable breakdown or irreconcilable difference with proper statutory separation)
    a. advantages – less expensive, emotional, don't have to prove up grounds
    b. disadvantages – sometimes less money
3. Fault
    a. adultery – voluntary intercourse w/ someone other than spouse b. bigamy – 1st wife has grounds for divorce (2nd may void)
    c. cruelty
        i. physical – a few acts
        ii. mental – too much/little sex
        iii. attempted murder – one act enough
    d. desertion – 1year, lease w/o consent of spouse e. drug addiction – 2 years showing a pattern
    f. insanity (NOT in IL)
    g. imprisonment (conviction of a felony)
    h. impotency
    i. venereal disease
4. Defenses to fault
    a. insanity (analogous to criminal law)
    b. collusion (agreement to simulate grounds)
    c. connivance (active enticement by so-called innocent party)
    d. condonation ((conditional) forgiveness) (like waiver)
    e. recrimination (both dirty)
    f. provocation
C. Economic aspects
    1. Before marriage antenuptial contracts are valid (as long as public policy ok)
        a. Statute of frauds – writing required
        b. consideration - found in the marriage
        c. fraud vitiates validity – need disclosure
    2. During marriage
        a. each spouse has duty to support the other
        b. as to 3rd parties, each spouse is independent (not responsible other's debt)
    3. After marriage
        a. contract is a valid separation agreement i. absent fraud or duress
            ii. non-modifiable except child support iii. writing required by statute
        b. decree – judge makes decision
            i. property
                (a) label and divide:
                    • separate: prior to marriage or by gift stays with individual includes appreciation

- marital: during marriage – includes pensions and tort recovery but not professional degrees
- (b) Distribute equitably (the marital property)
  - Background of parties (age education, ability to work)
  - Unilateral or bilateral source of assets
  - Liability of parties
  - Longevity of marriage
  - Standard of living of parties
  - Health of parties
  - Income of parties
  - Tax aspects
- (c) Non-modifiable
ii. Alimony (maintenance; spousal support) – No gender presumption
  - (a) amount – based on needs but can consider misconduct
  - (b) types
    - permanent – needs continuing but can be modified
    - rehabilitive
    - lump sum iii. Child support
  - (a) child is entitled to support until 18 or emancipated
  - (b) traditionally, death of parent terminates duty of support
  - (c) paternity
    - woman married: child presumes to be husband's
    - rebuttable except: USCACA
    - non-marital issue (entitled to "intermediate" equal protection. Test: important governmental interest (government burden) – cannot discriminate against kids
  - (d) Support (needs of child/ ability to pay)
    - modifiable, except: self induced, past due obligation
    - no tax aspects
D. Child Custody – fit parents have constitutional right
  1. Best interests of child
     a. Jurisdiction (Uniform Child Custody Jurisdiction and Enforcement Act)
  i. Home state
  ii. child and one parent have "significant connection"
  iii. abandons
  iv. no other states want
  v. Enforcement: Court that made initial determination has exclusive and continuing jurisdiction until neither child nor parent has significant connection with it.
  b. Factors
  i. Child's preference – more important in older kids ii. Health of parties
  iii. Involvement of parties
  iv. Proximity of relatives (siblings; grandparents)

                    v. Schools and institutions
             c. Shared – not statutorily presumed
             d. exclusive
                    i. can be physical custody or legal custody
                    ii. if exclusive, give other visitation e.
             modifiable
                    i. not final order (interlocutory)
                    ii. no full faith and credit
             f. "off the wall" – interest of the child
       2. Adoption
             a. Biological parents – rights are extinguished i.
                    voluntary
                    ii. involuntary
                           (a) parents' abuse, abandonment, or neglect
                           (b) procedural due process means notice and fair hearing
                           (c) unmarried father entitled to due process if:
                                  • acknowledges paternity in writing
                                  • involved with child
             b. adoptive parents (second step) – gain judicial sanction
                           (a) one-way street – only parents have duty to support not kids
                           (b) two-way street – inheritance

IV. Miscellaneous
  A. Surnames – wife need not adopt name – hyphenated names must be changed in
  court
  B. Torts – abolish spousal immunity
  C. Crimes
  D. 3rd person entices spouse away – can sue for alienation of affection
  E. Marvin/Hewitt (palimony)
       1. Not married they break up (no common law marriage) wants support
       2. Proposed solution
             a. implied contract from conduct
             b. consideration of sex is void as illegal
       3. Actual solution – constructive contract, contract implied in law, quasi contract
             a. benefit conferred b.
             expectation
             c. unjust to retain
  G. Artificial Insemination
       1. Easy case – anonymous sperm (never on bar)
       2. Surrogacy
             a. husband who consents to surrogacy is irebuttably bound
             b. formal termination of surrogates rights – father required
       3. In vitro
             a. easy case – donated sperm
             b. surrogacy – state makes no provision
             c. "property" – relative interests of parties are to be weighed

Federal Jurisdiction and Procedure

I. Subject Matter Jurisdiction
   A. Federal Courts are courts of limited jurisdiction
   B. Two primary jurisdictional bases:
      1. Arising under federal law if the claim is either: 1) created under federal law, or 2) if it merely depends on a substantial federal question.
      2. Diversity and an amount which exceeds 75,000
         a. Complete jurisdiction menas that no single Π may be a citizen of the same state of any Δ.
         b. Citizenship: individuals = home plus intent, corp. = business/incorporation
         c. unincorporated association = every member's domicile counts d. aliens can sue with diversity a non-alien
   C. Supplemental Jurisdiction
      1. Rule: If there is a primary jurisdictional basis for one claim, but not for the other claim, the federal court nonetheless has discretion to assert supplemental jurisdiction over both claims if they derive from a common nucleus of operative fact. (except diversity)
   D. Removal
      1. Rule: Δ's may remove an action from state court to federal court so long as there is fed. Jurisdiction over the removed claims.
      2. Exception: In removal where the only jurisdictional basis is diversity, there can be no removal if any single Δ is a citizen of a state where filed
   E. Erie Doctrine
      1. Conflict involving fed. Statute – Federal law governs
      2. No fed statute – state law governs

II. Personal jurisdiction and service of process in federal court (AWASP) A. Unless statute provides for jurisdiction, court borrows state law B. Service of process in federal court. Proper methods:
      1. **a**bode
      2. **w**aiver
      3. **a**gent service
      4. **s**tate methods
      5. **p**ersonal service
   C. Process is constitutional if it is reasonable calculate to apprise interested parties of litigation.

III. Venue
   A. Rule: Venue is proper in a district where either:
      1. any Δ resides, if all Δ reside in the same state
      2. any substantial part of the claim arose
   B. Transfer: move must be proper and is up to discretion

IV. Pleadings
   A. General requirements: Federal courts are a notice pleading regime therefore in federal court pleadings need only contain sufficient information to place the advertising in notice of claims and defenses being asserted but in fed. ct. fraud claims require particularity.
   B. Responsive pleadings waived unless consolidated together in first responsive

pleading within 20 days of service or 60 days if waiver:
   1. motion to dismiss for lack of personal jurisdiction
   2. motion to dismiss for improper service of process
   3. any motion challenging venue
C. Amendments (changes to complaints and answers)
   1. General Rule: Amendments shall be granted freely to do justice and to serve the merits.
   2. Relation back of amendments
      a. new claims: relate back in time if they derive from the same transaction of occurrence
      b. new parties: claims must arise from same occurrence or transaction & brand new party must have knowledge that but for mistake they would have been named within 120 days

V. Joinder
   A. Claims: Π may file as many claims as Π has against Δ
   B. Parties: may join parties if the claims involve the same transaction or occurrence
   C. Multi-party, multiforum, jurisdictional act - All persons having a claim arising from a single accident at a single, discrete location at which at least 75 people have died, may join as plaintiffs so long as any single Π is citizen of different state
   D. Counterclaims: claim filed by the Δ against Π
      1. Permissive: counterclaim that does not derive from the same transaction or occurrence as Π's claim
      2. Compulsory: counterclaim that does not derive from the same transaction or occurrence, must file or it is waived
   E. Impleader: 3rd party claims ok so long as new Δ may be liable to the Δ for all or part of Π's claim
   F. Interpleader: holder of common fund may join as Δs every rival fund claimant
   G. Intervention: act of non-party trying to intervene in suit
      1. As of right: absolute right if interest not protected by existing parties
      2. Permissive: court has discretion
   H. Indispensable parties: non-party that cannot be joined and whose absence is so prejudicial to existing party rights that the entire action must be dismissed
   I. Class actions
      1. Definition: An action where a named Π represents a class of commonly situated absent parties.
      2. Certification for class action:
         a. Commonality of issues of fact or law pertaining to the class b. Adequacy of named Π and class counsel found by judge

        c. Numerousity – class so numerous joinder is impracticable d. Typicality – named Π's claims are typical of the class

    3. If seeking money:

        a. predominance – common issues must predominant

        b. superiority – must show class action is superior method c. notice must be reasonable calculated to apprise of rights

VI. Discovery – proper if method and scope.

    A. Methods

        1. Automatic prompt disclosure each side must without awaiting any discovery request automatically

            a. all potentional supports witnesses b. all relevant supporting documents c. a damages computation

            d. insurance coverage

        2. Presumptive limits: only 10 depos per side & only 7 hours each

        3.. Duty to supplement – automatic and ongoing

    B. Scope – must be relevant and not privileged

        1. Relevant – need not be admissible at trial (broad and liberal)

        2. Not privileged (work-product)

            a. work product is material prepared for litigation

            b. Attorney's mental impression never! – Everything else with show of substantial need

VII. Trial and related motions

    A. Summary judgment will be granted if there is no genuine issue of material fact B. Judgment as a matter of law (directed verdict): after motion filed burden transfers to the non-moving party to show there is feminine issue of fact for trial C. Renewed motion for a judgment as a matter of law (JNOV): there must have been an original motion; granted if there was an insufficient evidentiary basis from which any reasonable jury could find for non-moving party

    D: New Trial: will be granted in courts discretion if: (1) there were errors affecting the parties substantial trial rights or the verdict was merely against the manifest weight of the evidence

    E. Right to trial by jury:

        1. must file written demand within 10 days of service of last pleading

        2. If seeking money constitutional right to trial by jury

VIII. Finality and appellate review

    A. finality (res judicata and collateral estoppel)

        1. res judicata: claim which has been full and fairly adjudicated to a final judgment on the merits cannot be relitigated

        2. collateral estoppel: issue which has been fully and fairly litigated as part of a final judgment on the merits cannot be relitigated by parties

        3. Finality rule: parties are barred from relitigating claims

4. Offensive collateral estoppel: a non-party can use judgment against party

B. Appellate jurisdiction: appellate courts are courts of appellate jurisdiction

    1. As a rule any final orders may be appended to the appellate court

    2. Exceptions

        a. partial final order: order resolving some claims – must allow instant appeal

        b. discretionary appeal of interlocutory order if both the district and appellate court certify:

            i. doubt on the order

            ii. controlling legal issue such that

            iii. appellate review would materially advance the litigation

Secured Transactions

I. Mechanics
    A. Security interest – right to keep or sell collateral to satisfy debt
      B. Collateral – property subject to the security interest:
        1. consumer goods – family purpose
        2. farm products
        3. inventory – business: use, sale or lease
        4. equipment – long term business use (catchall)
            • if something is/was used in another manner check, "primary use test" & "original use test"
            • software – test: Embedded means so firmly affixed thereto as to be considered part thereof. If so, the software is part of the goods for all purpose. If not, the software is a general intangible.
                • Farm products become inventory when processed
        5. instruments
        6. documents of title
        7. accounts – right to payment insufficient to be chattel paper
        8. deposit accounts (bank)
        9. health care insurance receivables
        10. chattel paper – test: writing(s) evidencing (1) obligation and (2) security instrument
        11. electronic chattel paper
        12. letter of credit right
        13. commercial tort claims
        14. general intangibles
        15. investment property
        16. Proceeds + proceeds thereof
    C. Between debtor and creditor (secured party)
        STEP ONE CREATION
        1. possession *or*
        2. security agreement
            a. authenticated record b. signed by debtor
            c. describing collateral d. control
        STEP TWO ATTACHMENT
        1. secured party must give value
        2. debtor must have rights in collateral
            a. after-acquired property clause b. exceptions
                i. 10-day rule for additional security for consumer goods ii. commercial tort claims
            c. future-advance clause
    D. Between creditor and others (subsequent purchasers, creditors, etc)
        STEP THREE PERFECTION

1. filing
    a. What?
    b. Where?
    c. How long?
2. possession
3. control
    a. deposit accounts
    b. letter of credit rights c. investment property
4. automatic
    a. PMSI in consumer goods b. assignment of accounts
    c. sale of payment intangibles or promissory notes d. security interests in investment property)
5. temporary (four months or twenty days)

II. Priorities

A. Secured party vs. lien creditor – secured party wins if perfected (bankruptcy lien creditor wins if old debt and 90 days) (20 day grace period for PMSI)

B. Perfected Secured Party v. Purchaser
1. consumer purchaser to consumer purchase purchaser prevails (i.e. takes free of claim of secured party) unless filing (automatic perfection is ineffective)
2. business purchaser 0 secured party prevails (automatic perfection is effective)
3. (BIOC) purchaser from a business – purchaser wins even if filing by secured party
4. HDC Rule
    C. Secured party v. secured party – first to file or perfect.
1. Except:
    a. PMSI – inventory (and chattel paper or instrument proceeds)
                i. notice
                ii. no grace
    b. PMSI – Equipment (and proceeds)
                i. grace
                ii. no notice
    c. purchaser of chattel paper (with possession) takes priority over non-possessory secured party as proceeds of inventory
2. with investment property, secured party with control prevails over secured party who filed
3. Priority in proceeds
4. fixtures and accessions a. fixtures
    b. accessions

III. Rights Upon Default (watch for waiver)

A. Secured party gets rights against debtor and other obligors
B. Possession and disposition by secured party
                    1. Possession
              a. self-help b. replevin
                    2. Disposition
              a. commercial reasonableness b. form of
              notification
                                i. to whom ii. contents
                                    a. non consumer goods b. consumer goods
C. Noncompliance
        1. damages plus 500 for each case on noncompliance
        2. Consumer goods: 10% of purchase price and interest
D. Acceptance of collateral in satisfaction
        1. non consumer goods – ok w/ voluntary turnover and debtor pays difference
        2. consumer goods – turnover has to be full satisfaction
E. Application of proceeds sale
        1. Expenses of retaking, holding, preparing, etc (incl. atty fees)
        2. satisfaction of obligation secured by security interest
        3. satisfaction of obligation secured by subordinate security interest
        4. debtor or trustee

Suretyship

I. Definition – A contract where one (surety) assumes the obligation of another
    A. Distinguish between (contract and surety)
        1. compensated – paid to provide surety (construction)
        2. gratuitous – done without compensation (co-signer) a. current: if done at same time = consideration b. non-current: if done later
            1) Nonnegotiable = not bound for lack of consideration
            2) Negotiable = bond as signed (indorser or maker) B.
    Distinguish between (types of liability):
        1. Surety – primary obligor (e.g. accommodation maker – signed on face)
        2. guarantor (of payment) – secondary obligor (e.g. accommodation indorser – signed on back)
        3. guarantor of collectibility – guarantor of collection (must use those words)
    C. statute of frauds applies to all types of suretyship (surety is bound through oral promise if the main purpose of the surety's promise is to benefit the surety)
    D. Arising by operation of law – where third party contracts with debtor to pay creditor and there is no novation, the original debtor becomes a surety by operation of law

II. Rights of Surety
    A. Against creditor – no rights except to pay (obligation)
        1. no notice requirement
        2. no requirement of surety to try to collect from debtor first
        3. surety cannot require to utilize security first except when debtor is bankrupt
        4. surety cannot designate which debt the creditor must credit
    B. Against debtor
        1. exoneration (suit to compel payment)
        2. subrogation (if total satisfaction; derived creditor right)
        3. reimbursement (indemnification) C.
    Against Co-Sureties (arises by contract)
        1. Exoneration (suit to compel payment) – suit to get other surety to pay portion
        2. subrogation (if total satisfaction of debt)
        3. contribution – action to get back anything paid that is more than fair share

III. Defenses of Surety
    A. Debtor's defenses
        1. yes - fraud or duress (unclean hands)
        2. No – infancy, insanity, bankruptcy
    B. Variation of Risk

1. Types – alteration of contract, extension of time, release of security, release of co-surety, impairment of collateral, etc
2. Effect
   a. gratuitous surety – total discharge
   b. compensated surety (Article 3, UCC) – discharge to the extent you can show a lose as a result of the variation (fact based)

Torts

INTENTIONAL TORTS

I. **Intent**
   a. General- if individual has knowledge with substantial certainty that harm will result
   b. Specific- purposely do something that causes harm
      i. Actor→ intent → causation → harm
   c. ***Brown v. Kendall*** – P interferes with two dogs fighting, hits D with a stick accident.
      i. ***Burden of proof is on the P*** – P must show intention was unlawful or D was at fault
   d. ***Cohen v. Petty*** – man driving faints, crashes car, and has no previous health issues.
      i. One who is suddenly stricken by illness he had no reason to anticipate is not liable for those he injures as a result of the illness. **P must prove D's conduct was unreasonable**
      ii. **RULE: D must act volitionally**
      iii. D must have **purposeful intent & knowledge with substantial certainty** that harm will occur
   e. ***Spano v. Perini***- D's blasting for construction causes damage to garage and car of P
      i. *Strict liability*- **even if you exercise due care, can be held liable for damages when engaging in dangerous action (i.e. blasting)**
   f. ***Garret v. Dailey*** – child pulls chair out from under adult causing injury
      i. Intent does not require malice.
      ii. RULE: intent for commission of intentional tort is present when person acts, knowing with substantial certainty that the harmful contact will occur
         1. Reasonable person of any age can know with substantial certainty
         2. D must act volitionally to be held liable. There is an age where a minor is too young to form intent
   g. RST § 8a – Intent (***majority rule)*** – the actor desires to cause consequence of his act or believes that the consequences are substantially certain to result from it
   h. RTT § 1 – intent – a person acts with the intent to produce consequence if (a) the person acts with the purpose of producing that consequence or (b) the person acts with knowledge of substantial certainty
   i. **RULE—Egg-shell skull** (or thick-skull rule): an individual is liable for all consequences resulting from her activities leading to an injury of another person, even if the victim suffers unusual damages due to a pre-existing vulnerability or medical condition.
      i. **Intent does not require a showing of malice, intent to injure, or other bad motive.** (Holding)
   j. ***Spivey v. Battaglia*** - man joking with female coworker, grabs her neck and pulls it towards him, paralyzing her on the left side. Statute of limitations for battery so sucs for negligence
      i. D was not substantially certain his actions would cause harm, no intent so no Battery
      ii. Intent - Where a **reasonable man** would believe that a particular result was substantially certain to follow
   k. **Substantial Factor Test**
      i. **If conduct was not a tort but a substantial factor in causing harm D will be liable**
      ii. **If conduct was a tor and was a substantial factor in harm, D will be liable**

         iii. **Policy Implications : Test recognized existence of a higher degree of responsibility for those who commit intentional torts v. those who act negligently**

l. ***Ranson v. Kitner-*** D's were hunting wolves accidently shot and killed P's dog b/c they thought it was a wolf
        i. ***Mistake does not negate intent***

m. ***McGuire v. Almy*** – P was nurse for D. D was mentally insane. D struck P with leg of a chair in midst of a violent outburst
        i. ***Mentally insane held to same standard of liability as anyone else***
            1. ***Mentally ill cannot be held liable if tort requires formation of malice***

n. ***Talmage v. Smith*** – Boys climbing on mans shed. He throws stick at them to scare them away, hits boy in the eye blinding him.
        i. D is liable for damages under **Transferred intent** (doesn't apply to IIED)
        ii. Transferred intent- when intent to cause harm to one person results in harm to another, not the intended target, law transfers intent to the person harmed

o. Intent Summary
        i. When an actor desires (specific) or has knowledge with substantial certainty (general) as to the consequences following
        ii. Does not require – malice, intent to injure, any other bad motive
        iii. Requires a volitional act (not negated by infancy, mental ability, mistake, intoxication)

II. Battery

a. **Cole v. Turner –** sets out elements of battery
        i. **Crowed world-** if two pass by each other w/o violence or harm, and one touches another or bushes up against them there is no battery
        ii. **The least touching of another in anger is battery**
        iii. **Offends a reasonable sense of personal dignity**

b. **Elements – P must show the D**
        i. Acted with intent to cause
        ii. Harmful or offensive contact with another or 3rd person or an imminent apprehension of such contact
        iii. a harmful contact with another person or a 3rd party occurs directly or indirectly
        iv. **without consent or lacking privilege**

c. ***Wallace v. Rosen*** – D tried to get P to move during a school fire drill by touching her back, P alleges D pushed her down the stairs
        i. **Intentionally touching another person is not battery if it doesn't occur in a rude, insolent or angry manner**
        ii. **Objective Standard** - would the ordinary, reasonable person, find the conduct offensive, NOT "did this particular P find the conduct offensive"

d. ***Fisher v. Carrousel Motor Hotel, Inc.*** – employee of D grabbed plate from the hand of P claiming a "negro could not be served in the club." P was not actually touched or physically harmed.
        i. The intentional grabbing of the plate constitutes battery - the touching element can be satisfied by contact with items that are connected with the body and are customarily regarded as part of their person (i.e. knocking a hat off of someone's head)

e. DAMAGES (require commission of an intentional tort)
        i. Nominal – if P has not suffered any actual pecuniary harm, awarded for deterrence

      ii. Compensatory (actual)- if P has suffered actually pecuniary harm, court was compensate for proven injury or loss

      iii. Punitive – if D's conduct was outrageous or malicious court may award damages to P in order to punish the D for his actions

  f. BATTERY REVIEW

      i. To prove a prima facie case for Battery, P must show D acted volitionally with intent to cause either harmful or offensive contact that resulted directly or indirectly in a harmful contact without the P's consent and lacking privilege

          1. Inoffensive contact is not battery

      ii. Liability for battery may attach even if the motive was benign, the P was unconscious during the touching, P was not actually touched but an item intimately associated was or the P was placed in imminent apprehension

III. Assault

An unlawful attempt to commit a battery, incomplete by reason of some intervening cause, which causes the victim to have imminent apprehension

  a. Elements – P must prove D

      i. Acted to cause an **imminent apprehension** in the P

      ii. Of harmful or offensive physical contact

      iii. Without consent or lacking privilege

  b. *I de S et ux v. E de S.* – man came at night demanding alcohol; P stuck her head out the window to say they were closed. D stuck the door with a hatchet but did not strike the woman

      i. *P may recover for assault even if no harm was done – Was P placed in imminent apprehension and was the apprehension reasonable?*

  c. *Western Union Telegraph Co. v. Hill* – Employee of P told wife of D to come behind the counter and he would pet her and love her. He reached for her but she jumped back.

      i. **Any act that excited an apprehension of a battery may constitute an assault** BUT D's act must amount to an offer to use force and there must be an **apparent ability** and **opportunity** to carry out the threat **imminently.**

  d. REVIEW OF ASSUALT

      i. Recover even if no actual harm was done

      ii. Apparent not actual ability is required

      iii. Awareness is necessary

      iv. Not enough to qualify as an assault without an over act – leering, mere preparation, words alone, words that contradict gestures or actions, words that lack imminence

      v. Enough to qualify as an assault – apprehension or anticipation of contact, words with unlawful conditions, words about non-existent danger or dangerous condition

IV. False Imprisonment (F/I)

  a. **ELEMENTS –P must prove D**

      i. acted with intent to confine another person

      ii. to a bounded area

      iii. that person is either aware of confinement or harmed by confinement

      iv. without consent or lacking privilege

  b. *Big Town Nursing Home, Inc. v. Newman* – P was committed to nursing home, told he could leave at any time, but was confined by D. Attempted to escape and failed, was placed with drug addicts and alcoholics and at one point locked in a restraining chair

      i. *RULE*: F/I is the direct restraint of the phys. Liberty of one person by another w/o adequate legal justification

1. ***Length of time is irrelevant*** (only relevant in determining damages)
2. ***If there is a reasonable means of escape there is no F/I***
3. Reasonable means void if means of escape would cause embarrassment or shame to the individual

c. ***Parvi v. City of Kingston*** – P tried to break up a fight between brothers. Detained by police for being visibly drunk. D drove the P to an abandoned golf course against his will to "dry out." He wandered from the golf course onto a the NY State Thruway and was hit by a car and severely injured

    i. ***A P's recollection of previous consciousness of confinement is not required to make out a prima facie case for F/I***

        1. ***F/I is a dignitary tort, it is not suffered unless its victim knows of the dignitary invasion***

d. ***Hardy v. Labelle's Distributing Co.*** - D hired P as a sales clerk. P accused of stealing, detained by D but given opportunity to leave. P says she wants to stay and defend herself against accusation.

    i. F/I is the unlawful restraint of an individual against his/her will. P felt restrained but stayed to clear her name and was not unwillingly restrained

    ii. RULE: Two Key Elements of F/I

        1. The restraint of an individual against his will and the unlawfulness of such restraint

        2. The individual may be restrained by act or merely by words which he fears to disregard

    iii. Actionable Confinement – ways to bring Actionable Confinement Claim

        1. Actual or apparent physical barriers

        2. Submission to overpowering physical force

        3. Submission to threat to apply physical force

        4. Submission to duress other than threats of physical force

            a. Retention of P's property may provide the "restraint" necessary

        5. Taking person into custody under an asserted legal authority

e. ***Enright v. Groves*** – D see's P's dog not on a leash. P is in her car, D asks to see drivers license P refuses. D forcibly arrests her, takes her to jail and charges her with dog leash ordinance violation

    i. D lacked proper legal authority. Officer must have valid legal authority to effectuate an arrest upon the person believed to have committed an offense. His demand for her license was unlawful and her refusal was not an offense.

    ii. **RULE: F/I arises when one is taken into custody by a person who claims but does not have proper legal authority**

f. **Whittaker v. Sandford**- D offered P Passage to US on his yacht. Upon arrival at port D refused to give P a rowboat to reach the shore.

    i. F/I can lie even if D does not actually physically prevent the P from leaving b/c freedom of movement is limited

    ii. D breached promise to take active steps to release P and thus commits F/I

g. Review of F/I

    i. Exists unless there is a reasonable means of escape

    ii. Exists unless the person is aware of an available exit

    iii. Doesn't require a stationary structure

    iv. Requires close confinement

    v. Even though there may be a perfectly safe avenue of escape a person is not req. to take it if the circumstances make it offensive to a reasonable sense of decency or personal dignity

      vi. RULE: liability for F/I req. D commit an act that was intended to cause and did cause the P to be confined or restrained in a bounded area

      vii. Confinement is not complete if there is a reasonable means of escape and the P is aware of that escape

V. Intentional Infliction of Emotional Distress (IIED)

  a. Elements –P must prove D

      i. Conduct was outrageous and extreme

          1. Threshold- the conduct must go beyond all possible bounds of decency and not tolerable in a civilized community

          2. Recklessness – P must prove D either: (1) intended to cause severe emotional distress or (2) acted with reckless disregard

              a. Defined as deliberate disregard of a high degree of probability that actions will result in a particular harm

      ii. Was intentional or reckless

      iii. And caused severe emotional distress

          1. Movement away from phys. req. b/c the phys. manifestation is more prone to fraud

          2. Severe emotional distress can be authenticated by the outrageousness of the actor's conduct

      iv. Without consent or lacking privilege

          1. IIED is the only intentional tort for which RECKLESSNESS applies

          2. NO TRANSFERRED INTENT

  b. *State Rubbish Collectors Association v. Saliznoff* – D collected trash for Acme. P claims territory infringement tries to force D to pay, which he does. D testifies that P threatened him and it caused him to become ill from fright

      i. *RULE* – one who by extreme and outrageous conduct intentionally or recklessly causes a severe emotional distress to another is subject to liability for the emotional distress and for the bodily harm that results from the emotional distress

  c. *Slocum v. Food Fair Stores of Florida* – D's employee verbally assaulted P, which aggravated a heart condition and led to P's heart attack.

      i. Conduct must be so outrageous that the <u>reasonable</u> person could be cause "<u>severe</u>" emotional distress, not simply "mere" emotional distress

      ii. RULE: liability for conduct exceeding all bounds which could be tolerated by society and of a nature especially calculated to cause mental damage of a very serious kind

  d. *Harris v. Jones* – P sues D for making fun of his speech impediment which caused a nervous breakdown

      i. *Humiliation suffered was not so intense to qualify as "severe." IIED REQUIRES SEVERITY*

      ii. *RULE: liability for IIED*

          1. *Conduct must be intentional or reckless, extreme or outrageous*

          2. *There must be a causal connection between the wrongful conduct and the emotional distress*

          3. *Emotional distress must be severe*

          4. *Without consent or lacking privilege*

  e. *Taylor v. Vallelunga* –P witnessed D's beat her father, seeks damages for IIED suffered

      i. *Third Party Bystander Recovery Rule*

          1. *To prove a prima facie case for recovery for conduct directed at 3rd party P must prove:*

              a. *The element of IIED*

              b. *D's conduct was either directed at the P or the P is present*

              c. *P is a close relative or family member AND*

              d. *D is aware that the P is present*

VI. **Trespass to Land (T/L)**
   a. **Elements – P must prove D**
      i. **Acted with intent to enter the property of another**
      ii. **And did enter another's land**
      iii. **Without consent or lacking privilege**
   b. *Dougherty v. Stepp* – D entered onto the unenclosed land of P, surveyed land but did not mark any tress or cut bushes
      i. *Action for T/L can be maintained **WITHOUT PROOF OF ANY ACTUAL DAMGE**. Every unauthorized entry is unlawful and a T/L*
   c. *Bradley v. American Smelting and Refining Co.* – P sued for deposit of microscopic airborne particles of heavy metals by D on their property
      i. *RULE: if the intrusion interferes with the right to exclusive possession of property T/L applies. If intrusion is to the use and enjoyment of property T/L applies but Person must establish that damages suffered were actual and substantial*
      ii. Nuisance
         1. Private – substantial and unreasonable interference with an individual's private use or enjoyment of property they possess or have immediate right to possess – must be offensive, inconvenient, or annoying to an average person in the community
         2. Public – an act that unreasonable interferes with the health, safety or property rights of the community as a whole – severity of inflicted injury must outweigh the social utility value of D
   d. *Herrin v. Sutherland*- D fires a gun over P's land doing damage to his home and property
      i. *If a foreign object disturbs the airspace reasonably close to the surface of the land it will constitute a T/L*
      ii. RST § 159 – air travel is a trespass only if it enters into immediate reaches of the airspace next to the land and interferes substantially with the others' use and enjoyment of the land
      iii. State rights for T/L have been preempted by Fed Reg. to prevent companies (i.e. airlines) from being brought to court for C/A of T/L
      iv. Rule of Capture: for oil and gas, no liability for drainage of oil and/or gas so long as there is no trespass to the property line of the D
   e. *Rogers v. Board of Road Commissioners of Kent County* – D failed to remove a fence post on P's land used to keep snow off the road, P runs it over with his mowing tractor and is thrown from the vehicle, killing him.
      i. **There was proper justification for the entry and presence of the object on the land, however at the conclusion of that justification (snow melting, season ending) any injury that is inflicted by the present of the object, whether negligent or not, is a T/L**
   f. **Types of Trespass**
      i. **Continuing:** activity that can be discontinued or abated at any time. A trespass in the nature of a permanent invasion of another's rights, such as a sign that overhangs another's property
      ii. **Permanent:** interference or intrusion that does not have a ready means of elimination. Consists of a series of acts, done on consecutive days. That are of the same nature that are renewed or continued from day to day, so the acts in the aggregate form one indivisible harm (i.e. Brown-fields cannot be abated)
   g. REVIEW of T/L
      i. Occurs when the D intentionally:
         1. Enters the P's land, or remains on the O's land without the right to be there even if permission were initially granted or causes an object to enter the P's land w/o permission

VII. **Trespass to Chattels (T/C)**
   a. **Elements- P must prove**
      i. **An act of the D interferes with the P's right of possession in the chattel**
      ii. **The D indented to perform the act that interfered with their possession**
      iii. **The D was the legal cause or set in motion that which caused the interference and damages resulted**
      iv. **Without consent or lacking privilege**
   b. **Glidden v. Szybiak** – P bitten by D's dog while playing with the dog on the porch of a candy store, not at D's home.
      i. **Owner of a chattel must prove more than NOMINAL DAMAGES TO and INTENTIONAL INTERFERENCE WITH chattel in order to prevail in a C/A for T/C**
      ii. **Damages:** nominal damages will not be awarded for T/C
         1. if T/C amounts in a dispossess the loss of possession itself is deemed to be an actual harm
         2. court places dispossession in a different category, even if small or nominal damages occur one can still be held liable for T/C
      iii. RST § 218 – chattel is impaired as to its condition, quality or value or the possessor is deprived of the use of the chattel for a substantial time or bodily harm is thereby caused to the possessor or ham is caused to some person or thing in which the possessor has a legally protected interest
   c. *CompuServe Inc. v. Cyber Promotions, Inc.* – D's sent mass spam to P's accounts via P's server, clogging the bandwidth and slowing the system down
      i. An action will lie because the P's memory space is actual property that is harmed by the sending of mass emails or spam
      ii. **Mass interference with possessory interest may allow T/C, dispossession is not required, court allows mere interfering or intermeddling to constitute T/C**

VIII. **Conversion**
   a. **Elements –P must prove D**
      i. **Acts with intent to exercise dominion and control**
      ii. **Which seriously interferes with P's right of possession in the chattel**
      iii. **Required to the D to pay full market value**
   b. *Pearson v. Dodd*- Employees of D entered his office w/o permission removed documents, copied them, put them back unharmed, and gave copies to P who published the information.
      i. **Publication of info that does not amount to literary property absent actual physical dispossession of the documents does not amount to conversion**
   c. **Bona Fide Purchaser Rule** – bona fide purchaser of chattel may become a converter if the chattel was stolen from the true owner
   d. **Serious Interference**- if the D refuses to return the chattel when asked or alters the chattel D may be liable for conversion b/c D action so seriously interferes with P's chattel rights that it amounts to a claim of dominion and control on the D's part – longer the withholding period and more extensive the use of the chattel more likely conversion
   e. **What Can Be Converted** – property subject to conversion is ltd. to tangible personal property and intangibles that have been reduced from phys. form (i.e. promissory note) and docs. In which title to a chattel is merged (i.e. bill of lading or warehouse receipt)
   f. **Remedies** – Damages: P is entitled to damages for the fair market value of the chattel. The value is generally computed as of the time and place of the conversion. D is given title upon satisfaction of the judgment so that, in effect, there is a forced sale of the chattel. If the D wishes to return the chattel, the P is not obligated to accept it once the chattel has been converted

PRIVILEGES OR JUSTIFICATIONS

I.   **Consent**
  a.   Consent is offered as a defense to negate intent in P's prima facie case. 2 types:
  b.   **Explicit or Express consent** – words and actions of the P were explicit to warrant the P's consent to an action
  c.   **Implied consent** – words or deeds manifest consent to the D
      i.   Objective manifestation of consent – whether a reasonable person in the position of the D, observing P's action would have deemed it consensual
      ii. Real but Unmanifested consent – if the P subjectively consents and there is a way to prove it, the consent will be proven even if never manifested by D
      iii. Custom- if D can show that it was customary for one in the P's position to consent, regardless of manifestation there will be consent
      iv. Inaction – the P's inaction by itself is indicative of the existence of consent
      v.   **TEST: Whether a reasonable person in the D's position would have inferred by the P's action or inaction that consent had occurred**
  d.   ***O'brien v. Cunard S.S. Co.*** – surgeon employed by D vaccinated P on a ship, P had already been vaccinated and did not want to be vaccinated again, yet she held her arm out and didn't tell anyone she didn't want the shot. The D's surgeon gave the her shot
      i.   HOLDING: based on the P's over acts and surrounding circumstances, P consented and the surgeons acts were lawful. Consent is implied by P's conduct
      ii. **Consent can be implied by: (1) P's conduct (2) custom (3) other surrounding circumstances**
  e.   ***Hackbard v. Cinvinnati Bengals, Inc.*** - P hit in the back of the head during football game and injured intentionally – even though it was the custom of the game to hit eachother, this was extraordinary action that was outside of the rules and parameters of the game
  f.   ***Mohr v. Williams*** – P went to have ear surgery, D operated on the wrong ear while P was under anesthesia, operation was successful, P sues for battery
      i.   ***HOLDING***: If D's actions exceeded the consent given and the D does a substantially different act that the one authorized by P's consent D is liable
      ii. **RULE: you cannot operate without consent unless it is life-threatening.**
      iii. **EXCEPTIONS**
          1.   **Incapacitation – unable to give consent b/c unconscious or other reason**
          2.   **Emergency – necessary to save life or safeguard health and urgent**
          3.   **Lack of consent not indicated – no indication that consent would not be given were it possible**
          4.   **Reasonable person would consent in the circumstances**
      iv. Medical Providers Rule – treatment must be (1) necessary to prevent serious bodily harm and (2) it must be urgent – if there is time to seek consent then must wait
      v.   Withdrawal of consent
          1.   Patient must act or use language that (1) can be subject to no other inference (2) must be unquestioned responses from a clear reasonable mind
          2.   Must be medically feasible to stop treatment w/o detriment to patient
  g.   ***DeMay v. Roberts*** - DeMay was in the room when Robert's gave birth, she did not know he was not a doctor and did not consent to having him in the room
      i.   ***HOLDING*** – consent that is obtained through misrepresentation is invalid
  h.   Invalidation of Consent
      i.   Exceeding scope – D's action goes beyond manifested consent by P
      ii. Mistake – if P expressly consented by mistake, consent is valid defense for D but Invalid if D caused mistake or knows of mistake and takes advantage
      iii. Induced by fraud – if induced by fraud, GENERALLY not a defense. Fraud must got an essential matter, if collateral matter consent remains effective

        iv. Consent obtained by duress may be held to be invalid – threats of future action or some future economic deprivation do not constitute sufficient legal duress

        v. Lack of capacity – intoxicated persons, unconscious persons, minors, mentally handicapped/incompetent lack capacity

        vi. Criminal activity

            1. MAJORITY – cannot give consent to a criminal act consent always invalid

            2. MINORITY – can consent to a criminal act for purposes of tort liability

            3. EXCEPTION- where the specific purpose of the law is to protect victims of a protected class, consent cannot be given and will not be accepted

II. Self Defense

a. **RULE: D is privileged to use reasonable force to defend himself against unprivileged acts that the D reasonably believes will cause bodily harm or offensive contact, court uses an objective standard in determining S/D**

b. **Reasonable belief** – actor need only have a reasonable belief as to other party's actions, reasonable mistake as to the existence of the danger does not deny defense

c. **Reasonable mistake** – S/D may be used when real threat of harm and where D reasonably believes there is one –subjective belief is not sufficient – objective basis for belief required

d. **Unjustified Use of Force** – D's unusual, irrational fears or belief that an attack is imminent w/o evidence does not justify attack on another especially w/ deadly force

e. **Justified Use of Force** – D is privileged to respond to an apparent threat of attack by P even if P never intended to attack at all – mistaken perception of an attach will warrant reasonable use of force as long as a reasonable person would have perceived a threat

f. Retaliation – S/D is only limited to the right to use force to prevent the commission of a tort

g. Preemption – S/D may not be used to justify striking another who threatens no immediate injury

h. **Duty to Retreat**

        i. **MAJORITY – D may stand ground and use deadly force against an attack even if the D could retreat with complete safety**

        ii. **MINORITY – D who is attacked must retreat if it can be safely done**

        iii. **EXCEPTIONS: (1) a person does not have a duty to retreat from an assault in one's own home or while in his place of business (2) when effecting a lawful arrest, police have no duty to retreat**

i. **Existence of Privilege** – anyone is privilege to use reasonable force to defend himself against a threatened batter on the part of another, privilege is unavailable to the aggressor

        i. **If initial aggressor retreats and initial victim peruses the attack or uses unreasonable force aggressor is now privileged**

j. **Provocation**- insults, verbally threats, or opprobrious language doesn't justify S/D. provocation doesn't warrant battery but may limit damages. If abusive words are accompanied by an actual threat reasonably warranting assault one may be privileged to defend

k. **Liability to 3ʳᵈ party** – if in the course of reasonably defending himself, he accidently injures 3ʳᵈ party, still protected by S/D (may be liable for negligence) – deliberate injury to 3ʳᵈ party waives S/D

III. Defense of Others

a. Privilege- similar to S/D for 3ʳᵈ persons. Closest questions concern use of reasonable force

b. Intervention – D who intervenes to defend another must believe that the victim would have privilege of S/D

c. Reasonable Mistake

        i. MAJORITY –the intervenor "steps into the shoes" of the person being aided, if the person being aided had no privilege of S/D then the intervenor does not either

        ii. MINORITY – if the person being aided did not have the privilege of S/D intervenor would not be liable if he proved: (1) he reasonably believed that the person aided could have used force to protect himself and (2) reasonable force was used

IV. Defense of Property

a. *Kato v. Briney*- owners installed spring gun in vacant farm building, injured P

        i. *HOLDING*: the fact that an intruder is acting unlawfully does not justify maintenance of a mechanical device to protect property that can cause great physical injury. Device of this nature only permitted if intruder is committing a violent felony, endangering lives of the occupants

V. **Recovery of Property (Recapture of Chattels)**
  a. *Hodgden v. Hubbard* – P bought stove on credit, D's credit no good, catch P forced him to give stove back
    i. *HOLDING*: owner may recover chattels by force, when possession was obtained by fraud
      1. Owner must proceed (1) w/o unreasonable delay (fresh pursuit) (2) w/o reasonable use of force (must first request return of chattels then can engage in use of force)
  b. **RULES:**
    i. **Where another's possession of the chattel began lawfully, one may only use peaceful means to recover the chattel**
    ii. **Force may be used to recapture the chattel only when in hot pursuit of one who has obtained the possession unlawfully**
  c. Limitations on Privilege
    i. Fresh or hot pursuit
    ii. Reasonable force under circumstances
    iii. Timely demand to recover chattel before use of force unless futile or dangerous
    iv. Recovery only from tortfeasor or 3rd party who knows or should know chattels tortuously obtained
    v. Use of force to recover chattels form an innocent 3rd person invalidates privilege
  d. Entry on Land to Recapture - if on wrongdoers land, or an innocent 3rd party's property, owner may enter and reclaim the chattel if (1) in a reasonable time & (2) reasonable manner (peaceful manner for 3rd party)
    i. Owner lacks privilege if the chattel is on another's land b/c of the owner's own fault
  e. *Bonkowski v. Arlan's Department Store* –P was detained in a store by a office when she was accused by a 3rd party of theft. She produced receipts and was released
    i. *HOLDING:* if the shopkeeper or the agent thereof reasonably believes the individual has unlawfully taken goods held for sale in the shopkeeper's store then the shopkeeper or agent enjoys the privilege to detain that individual for a reasonable investigation
    ii. *RULE:* a shopkeeper's privilege exists to detain a customer for a reasonable investigation if the shopkeeper has reason to suspect that the customer has stolen goods

VI. **Necessity**
  a. Public – where the act if for the public good, the necessity is absolute
  b. Private – where the act is solely to benefit any person or to protect any property from destruction or serious injury the defense is qualified as necessity
  c. *Surocco v. Geary* **(Public Necessity)** – P's home was destroyed to stop the spread of a fire by D who was fire marshal in San Fran. D claimed public necessity
    i. *HOLDING*: the right to destroy property is justified if it is done to prevent fire or other disaster from proliferating and is done in the good-faith belief that it is a necessity
  d. *Vincent v. Lake Erie Transp. Co.* **(Private Necessity)** – D's steamship was on P's dock, while unloading a storm came, boat stayed in port and damaged P's dock.
    i. *HOLDING*: the private necessity of avoiding either destruction or damage to one's property gives rise to a privilege to invade the property rights of another BUT privilege is limited to the entry, and compensation for any resulting damages must be made
    ii. *RULE*: **a person may interfere w/ the real or personal property of another where the interference is reasonably and apparently necessary to avoid threatened injury from a natural or other force where the threatened injury is substantially more serious than the invasion undertaken to avert it**

VII. Authority of Law

a. Act done under authority of law is privileged (i.e. police officer executing a valid arrest warrant and using proper procedure has a defense against false imprisonment)

VIII. Privilege of Arrest
   a. Arrest w/ warrant – office is privileged if the court has jurisdiction to issue a warrant, warrant is fair on its face, and officer uses proper procedures in making the arrest
   b. Warrantless arrest
      i. Felony or breach of peace in presence – an office may make a warrantless arrest for a felony or breach of the peace which is being committed or seems about to be committed in officer's presence (private citizen may also do the same)
      ii. Past Felony – an officer may make warrantless arrest, provide that officer reasonably believes that the felony has been committed and also reasonably believes that he has the right criminal
      iii. Citizen's arrest – valid only if a felony has in fact been committed, citizen won't lose privilege by arresting the wrong person provided the citizen reasonably believes the person to be the right one

IX. Discipline
   a. persons charged w/ maintaining discipline sometimes privileged to use force/restraint to ensure discipline (i.e. teachers, parents, military officials)

X. **Justification**
   a. *Sindle v. New York City Transit Authority* - P was on school bus owned by D, several students vandalized bus, D failed to stop and drove them to the police station
      i. *HOLDING:* an individual may assert a defense of justification when the D's action were reasonable and done to protect others from personal injury or to protect property

NEGLIGENCE

Omission to do something a reasonably prudent person would do or doing something which a reasonably prudent person would not do

I. **Elements of Negligence**
   a. **Duty – a legal duty requiring the D hold himself to a certain standard of care**
      i. **Standard of Care – D acts as a reasonably prudent person in the same or similar circumstances**
         1. **Physical characteristics (blind, deaf, amputee) changes standard of care – mental illness not counted**
         2. **Child Standard- child of like age, intelligence and experience unless child is engaged in adult activity**
         3. **Professional Standard – ordinary member of profession has lower standard than specialists**
         4. **Negligence Per Se – standard of care can be established by statute ordinance or regulation, allows court to bypass Duty and Breach via black letter law**
   b. **Breach - D fails to meet the standard of care**
      i. **Direct breach**
      ii. **Circumstantial – i.e. slip and fall**
      iii. **Constructive notice – was the D aware**
      iv. **Res Ipsa Loquitur – the thing speaks for itself – common law use of circumstantial evidence**
   c. **Causation**
      i. **Cause in fact – P's injury is caused by the D's conduct**
      ii. **"But-For" the D's conduct the P would not have suffered the harm**
      iii. **Proximate Cause – D's conduct must be shown to be the proximate or reasonably significant cause of the P's harm**

d. **Damages- P suffered a cognizable injury**
e. RULE – liability for negligence – **D has duty to prevent a foreseeable harm to P and breached** that duty **by failing to exercise due care and breach** of the duty **was the actual and proximate cause of the harm**
f. Contributory Negligence – conduct on part of the P which falls below the standard of conduct to which he should conform for his own protection and is a legally contributing cause cooperating with the negligence of the D in bringing harm to the P
    i. MAJORITY – Contributory negligence is an affirmative defense that D must raise and prove
    ii. MINORITY – P is required to prove that he is not contributorially negligent
    iii. C/L – if the P was contributory negligent at all they would not win
    iv. Comparative Negligence – compares negligence of P to D then subtracts damages accordingly
g. *Lubitz v. Wells* – D left a golf club out in backyard, D's son swung at a stone on the ground and stuck P
    i. *HOLDING:* a person is not negligent if there is little possibility that his conduct will injure another. The chance that D's son would injure P was not foreseeable
    ii. *RULE:* reasonable conduct w/ a low probability of harm is not negligent. The foreseeable risk of injury was remote given the reasonable conduct
h. *Blyth v. Birmingham Waterworks Co.* – D installed water mains on the street which burst when they froze on a record cold winter and damaged P's home.
    i. *HOLDING:* negligence involves the creation of an unreasonable risk, by act or omission, which a reasonably prudent person would not create
        1. extreme circumstances so D not liable – must protect against average no extraordinary
        2. that which is reasonably unanticipated the D cannot be held liable for
    ii. *RULE: the objective reasonable person under similar circumstances*
i. *Gulf Refining Co. v. Williams* – P severely burned by explosion from opening a drum of gasoline purchased from D
    i. *HOLDING:* possibility of harm must be such that it would induce a person of ordinary care to change his course of action to avoid the anticipated harm
    ii. *Threat of Serious Injury* – more serious the potential injury, less probable its occurrence need by before D will be held liable for not guarding against it – cannot have excessive burden of care
j. *Chicago B & Q.R. Co. v Krayenbuhl*- P injured by railroad turntable that was unlocked and unguarded D's rules required the turntable to be locked when not in use
    i. *HOLDING*: to determine negligence you must consider
        1. *Character and location of the premises*
        2. *Purpose for which the premises are used*
        3. *Probability of injury*
        4. *Precautions necessary to prevent such injury and*
        5. *Relationship such precautions bear to the beneficial use of the premises*
    ii. *Attractive nuisance doctrine* – a person who owns property on where there is a dangerous thing or condition that will foreseeably lure children to trespass has a duty to protect those children from danger
    iii. *Trespasser Rule* – property owner has no duty to act in anticipation of trespassers in the absence of a pre-existing relationship – if presence of trespasser is known then duty arises
        1. D will satisfy duty by simply warning trespasser of dangerous condition
        2. Duty exists when, property owner creates the danger, the anger arises from a natural condition or the owner has constructive or actual notice of trespasser

3. If the owner knows that part of his land is frequented by trespassers must use reasonable care to make the premises safe or warn of the dangers
4. Owner must exercise reasonable care for the trespassers safety if trespassers land use becomes customary or a pattern

k. ***Davidson v. Snohomish County***- P suffered injuries and wrecked car while crossing bridge in D's county
   i. ***HOLDING***: there is no duty on the part of a public body to assume the burden of safeguarding against all conceivable accidents P's were ***Contributorially negligent***

l. ***U.S. v Carroll Towing Co.*** – negligent act of D caused barge to break free from the pier and sink, P (US) seeks compensation for the cargo. Connors Co. seeks compensation for the barge
   i. ***HOLDING***- if the burden of preventing the injury is lower than the product of probably of its occurring and the amount of harm then there is a breach of duty of care and liability
   ii. ***JUDGE LEARNED HAND'S BALANCING TEST*** – BURDEN (B) < HARM (L) x PROBABILITY (P)

II. DUTY OF CARE

Failure to Act Cases

a. ***Hegel v. Langsom*** - P claims D let their college aged daughter become associated with criminals, drug users, allowed her to be absent from her dorm and failed to return her to her parents
   i. ***HOLDING:*** colleges and universities are under no affirmative duty to regulate the private lives of students. expected students have the necessary maturity to care for themselves w/o supervision

b. ***L.S. Ayers & Co. v. Hicks***- P got fingers caught in an escalator. D unreasonably delayed stopping it
   i. ***HOLDING***: an invitor or one who has control of an instrumentality that causes harm to another has a legal duty to rescued that other person even if he is not negligent – owner didn't cause the harm their liability lies in their misfeasance

c. ***J.S. and M.S. v. R.T.H.*** – two girls sexually abused by neighbor. Girls' parents bring action against abuser's wife alleging negligence for failure to act
   i. ***TEST for DUTY:*** (1) foreseeability, (2) public policy implications (3) whether D has the ability to control the opportunity to prevent such harm and (4) responsibility to prevent or warn of harm
   ii. ***HOLDING:*** when a spouse has actual knowledge or special reason to know of a behavior towards another, spouse has duty of care to take reasonable steps to prevent or warn of the harm. A breach of such a duty constitutes proximate cause of the resultant injury. Must be determined under the totality of the circumstances considering risk of harm and practicality of prevention

d. ***Tarasoff v. Regents of the University of California***- a patient at the University Psych Hospital told Doctor of intent to kill P, Police detain patient but eventually release him, two months later he kills P
   i. ***HOLDING:*** doc bears a duty of reasonably care and warm potential victims about the known violent tendencies or intentions of a patient, doc does not need to prevent harm simply warn
   ii. ***RULE:*** one person owes no duty to control the conduct of another nor to warn those endangered by such conduct UNLESS D has a special relationship to the tortfeasor or the victim

e. Exceptions to Duty
   i. Based on (1) the nature of the P (2) the type of harm suffered or (3) the D's relationship to the P
   ii. Common Carriers & Innkeepers – C/l imposes a duty to assist patrons
   iii. Business Relationships – imposition of a duty to anyone who maintains a business, must furnish warning and assistance to a business visitor regardless of source of danger

     iv. Employer-Employee – employer must give warning or assistance to employee who is endangered or injured during the course of his employment

     v. D is involved in the injury – has a duty to warn and assist if danger or injury is due to D's conduct or an instrument under D's control

     vi. Joint Venture – when two persons engage in common pursuit, some courts impose duty on both

     vii. Assumption of Duty when D

          1. Voluntarily begins to render assistance even if under no legal obligation must use reasonable care

          2. D must make reasonable efforts to keep P save while P is in D's care

          3. D may not discontinue aid if doing so would leave P in a worse position prior

     viii. Duty to Control Others – D has undertaken to control 3rd party who subsequently injures the P. duty may arise from special relationship btwn P and D or D and 3rd party.

Owners and Occupiers of Land Cases

f.   On the Premises

     i.   **Trespassers**

          1. **One who intentionally and w/o consent or privilege enters another's property (no duty owed to unforeseeable trespassers)**

          2. **Knowledge of trespassers = duty**

          3. **Attractive nuisance = duty**

     ii.   **Licensees**

          1. **An individual who enters the premises of the owners by permission, but for the individual's own purposes (i.e. social guest), taking the premises of his host as he finds them.**

          2. **Must simply warm of that which you are aware of and make guests aware of**

          3. **The owner of a premises has a duty to warn the licensee of any hidden dangers which are unknown to his guest but which the owner has knowledge, and to refrain from injuring his guest willfully or wantonly**

     iii.   **Invitees**

          1. **An individual who goes on the land in furtherance of the owners business**

          2. **owner of the premises has a duty to exercise reasonable care in keeping the premises reasonable safe for use by the invitee**

     iv.   **Duty of Care**

          1. **Trespassers (lowest) → Licensees → invitees (highest)**

g. ***Salevan v. Wilmington Park Inc (Outside the Premises)*** – P sues after hit by foul ball near D's ballpark

     i. *HOLDING:* public has a right to safe use of highways and landowners many not interfere with this right though the use of their land. Landowner must take reasonable precautions to protect the travelling public from harm

h. ***Sheehan v. St. Paul & Duluth Ry. Co. (On the Premises- trespassers)*** – P got foot caught in rails of D's track while trespassing, oncoming train struck P and severed his foot

     i. *HOLDING:* landowner has a duty of care to trespassers but duty only arises when the Ry. Co. becomes aware of the danger. When aware of danger it must make all reasonable effort to prevent harm

     ii. *RULE:* railroad co. has the right to a free track in such places it is not bound to act or service in anticipation of trespassers, trespasser who enters onto the land for his own purpose assumes all of the risks of the conditions on the land

iii. **RULE: a land occupier owes a duty of care to a trespasser only after he or she has discovered the presence of the trespasser**
1. CAVEAT: landowner owes no duty to a trespasser to make land safe, warn of dangers , avoid carrying on dangerous activities, or to protect the trespasser in any other way
2. Common Law Rule: trespasser took the property as it existed upon entry onto the land, including concealed artificial or natural dangers
iv. Land occupier has no legal obligation to discover, remedy or even warn a trespasser of such dangers. **The only obligation was to refrain from willfully harming the trespasser** (i.e. spring guns)
1. Exceptions
   a. Frequent or known trespassers
      i. Frequent: actual or constructive knowledge an obligation to warn of hidden and serious dangers know to the land possessor may be imposed
      ii. Conditions on the land that a trespasser would be expected to discover or inherent in the use of the land → no warning necessary
      iii. Known: awareness of trespasser and knowledge that trespasser is approaching an artificial (man-made) condition → obligation to warn trespasser is there is danger of serious bodily harm or death
   b. Child trespassers
      i. Traditional view: trespassing children would be barred from recovery
      ii. Modern view: turntable doctrine → attractive nuisance doctrine → child land entrant doctrine ("child trespasser doctrine" (RST 39)
v. *Duty may arise if the railroad has constructive notice of trespassers presence*
i. *Barmore v. Elmore* – P went to D's house, D's son, who had a history of mental illness, stabbed P
   i. *RULE* – as to a licensee, the owner of a premises is only required to warm his guest of any hidden dangers which the owner has knowledge or awareness
j. *Campbell v. Weathers*- P entered D's business, P familiar with the store fell into an open trap door
   i. *HOLDING*: a regular or perspective customer of a place of business does not have to make a purchase on a particular occasion to be considered an invitee unless it appears the person had no intention of presently or in the future becoming a customer
   ii. *RULE* – a regular customer who enters a place of business is considered an invitee
      1. *Minority* – duty of affirmative care to keep business safe is cost of doing business
      2. *Majority* – basis of liability is representation implied when you encourage individuals to come on the property
   iii. Sales People and Job applicants – test is whether the visitor reasonably believes that premises have been held open to them for the particular purpose for which they enter
      1. CAVEAT – salesman paying unsolicited call to a private home is not an invitee at the outset b/c he cannot reasonably anticipate that the premises have been made safe for him

III. STANDARD OF CARE
Reasonable Person Standard

a. *Vaughn v. Menlove* – D built a hay rick on his land close to P's cottage, it caught fire and burned P's cottage, D know the rick was likely to ignite
   i. *HOLDING:* the objective standard of the prudence of an ordinary person applies

ii. ***RULE :*** the standard of care is founded upon the judgment of the person of ordinary prudence, not the subject judgment of the D, even though the judgment was based on an honest attempt to act reasonably
1. *Majority* – mental state so low it is considered imbecilic will relieve actor of negligence
2. *Minority* – mental status may not relieve the D of negligence and may not relieve the P from being contributorially negligent

b. ***Declair v. McAdoo-*** D tried to pass P on the road and D's tire blew out, he swerved and hit P's car
i. ***HOLDING***: every adult in the community is held to a general knowledge of certain acts, i.e. that worn tires are dangerous and shouldn't be used
ii. ***RULE***: every automobile drive and owner is charged with such knowledge of the safe condition of his car as can be ascertained via a reasonable inspection.
1. ***reasonable person pays attention and is not distracted UNLESS legitimate distraction***

c. ***Timarco v. Klein*** – P a tenant in D's apartment, injured when glass shower door shattered
i. ***HOLDING***: test of negligence is whether a party's conduct was reasonable under all the circumstances of a particular case. Evidence of custom and usage by other engaged in the same business bears on what is reasonable conduct
ii. **RULE: when proof of an accepted practice is accompanied by evidence that the D conformed to it, this may establish due care**
iii. **Majority** – the courts allow evidence of custom or usage for the purpose of showing either the presence or absence of reasonable care, this evidence is not conclusive it is a framework

d. ***Cordas v. Peerless Transportation Co.*** – taxi driver held at gunpoint abandons car and car hit pedestrian
i. ***HOLDING:* Emergency Doctrine -** a person in an emergency that demands prompt action is not required to exercise the same standard of care that is required in normal circumstances
ii. ***Emergency Doctrine Limitations – must arise suddenly and unexpectedly and not created by the actor***

Physical Handicaps

e. ***Roberts v. State of Louisiana-*** P fell after being run into by a blind man who was not using a cane
i. HOLDING: the <u>standard of care applicable to handicapped persons is that they must take those precautions that ordinary, reasonable persons would if they were similarly handicapped</u>
ii. **accepted physical handicap but not mental handicaps with exceptions**

f. ***Breunig v.Family Ins. Co.-*** woman had an insane delusion which affected her ability to drive car safely which led to an accident involving P, P sues woman's insurance company D
i. ***HOLDING:*** a sudden, unpredictable should not be treated under the general rule of insanity. It is injury to home someone responsible for conduct he is incapable of avoiding and which incapability was unknown prior the incident

Child Actor Standard

g. ***Robinson v. Lindsay*** –D was the child driver of snowmobile that severed the finger of P
i. ***HOLDING:*** where a child engages in an inherently dangerous activity, child is held to an adult standard of care, even though general rule is that a child is held to the standard of a reasonable child of like age, intelligence and experience

ii. ***Reasonable Child Rule*** – minors must act as a reasonable child of like age, intelligence, maturity, training and experience, with the exception of when a child is engaged in adult activities
    1. Under 6yr old - no liability
    2. 6-14yrs old - rebuttable presumption presume child is not negligent
    3. 14-18 yrs old- rebuttable presumption presume child can be negligent

Professional Standard

h. ***Heath v. Swift Wings, Inc.*** - D pilot acted negligently and crashed the plane, his estate brings action against D and expert testimony shows the D acted contrary to a reasonable person
    i. ***RULE:* the professional D's negligence may be shown through expert testimony**
        1. *If you are a professional you will be held to a minimum standard of care*
        2. *Specialists are held to a higher standard*
    ii. ***Expert Testimony* – must prove that D's conduct contrary to common school of thought**
        1. Must establish both the standard course of conduct in the profession and that D departed from that standard
        2. Knowledge, training and skill, or ability and competence of an ordinary member of the profession in good standing
    iii. Malpractice Liability – the professional is liable for malpractice only if he acted w/o the requisite minimum skill and competence
    iv. Exceptions – blatant negligence, obligation, must be a respected school of thought

Trusts

I. Creation of Private (NonCharitable) Trust

    A. Express Trust – created by language

        1. Definition: Fiduciary relationship wherein trustee holds legal title for the beneficiary, who hold equitable title

        2. Declaration of trust or transfer in trust

            a. Declaration: Settlor is trustee

            b. Transfer: Settlor is not trustee

        3. Elements (settler must put his TRIB in writing)

            a. Settlor with capacity (sane & 18)

            b. Trust purpose

                i. Anything legal

                    (a) support

                    (b) conserve assets

                    (c) save taxes

                ii. not against public policy

                    (a) destruction

                    (b) looking favorable upon divorce

                iii. If purpose bad, consider settler intent

                    (a) if have wanted trust without it, strike clause

                    (b) if he wouldn't, void the trust

            c. Res – specific identifiable property

            d. Intent – use language, name of settler

                i. precatory terms – insufficient

                ii. exception: detail (dollars – shows intent)

            e. Beneficiary – settler cannot be sole beneficiary

            f. writing

                i. inter vivos

                    (a) realty – writing (S of F)

                    (b) Personalty – no writing even oral

                ii. Testamentary

            g. Trustee

                i.. if necessary appointed by court

                ii. unlike regular agent, has legal title, and personal liability

    B. Resulting Trust = implied trust (arise from conduct)

        1. Purchase money

            a. by agreement

            b. by gift to someone not related (gift not intended)

            c. for close relatives, presume gift

        2. Failure of express trust

        3. Failure of charitable or honorary trust

    C. Constructive trust – to prevent unjust enrichment

II. Transfer of Interest

A. Restraints – are permitted

B. Illinois (where settler is not the beneficiary, automatic spendthrift provision)

    1. beneficiary cannot convey

    2. credit cannot attach except under court order

C. Discretionary – settler gives discretion to trustee to pay the life beneficiary not only the income, but also the corpus (principal)

    1. Before exercise – cannot be reached

    2. After exercise – can be reached

    3. Beneficiary cannot force distribution, unless he shows trustee acted in bad faith or in violation of duty

III. Termination

A. Presumption – when silent presume trusts irrevocable

B. Irrevocable trusts

    1. Settlor alive – if trustee, settler and all beneficiaries agree (consent) irrevocable trusts can be revoked

    2. Settlor dead – if all parties agree, and no trust purpose would be thwarted then irrevocable can be revoked

C. Illinois – statutory spendthrift provision would be thwarted – not revocable if dead

IV. Charitable

A. Perpetual – OK

B. Cy Pres - if specific charity is give to next closest

C. Honorary – beneficiary not charity or private (pets)

    1. Technically void(violates RAP)

    2. but, upheld if trustee willing

V. Administration

A. Investment standard ("prudent investment rule") – I IT LAN

    1. Income and safety

    2. Inflation

    3. Taxes

    4. Liquidity and diversification

    5. Appreciation

    6. Will beneficiary have other resources

B. Duties of trustee

    1. Duty to follow instructions (SAIL)

    2. Segregation of assets

    3. Impartiality to all beneficiaries

    4. Loyalty - can't do business w/ trust b/c supervision is impossible

    5. Accounting – keep records, pay on time

C. Liability of trustee

D. Uniform Principal and Income Act

    1. Principal (corpus) – repayments or loans – distributions, stock splits

    2. Income – rent, income, cash dividends

Personal Property (contracts, property, equity, family law)

I. Acquisition of possession or title
    A. Lost, Misplaced, unowned, trover
        1. Lost (found in a place where it shouldn't be) Goes to finder unless trespasser or private locus
        2. Misplaced (found in place where it should be) – goes to landowner
        3. Unowned – acquire possession with intent
        4. Trove (gold or silver in refined state) – treat like property (goes to finder)
    B. Bailments – giving off possession (not title) by bailor, it is to be returned
        1. defined: bailee must have intent to accept, item not accidentally left
        2. Types and results
            a. sole benefits or bailor, bailee liable for gross negligence
            b. sole benefit of bailee, bailee liable for slight negligence
            c. mutual benefit bailment; bailee liable for ordinary negligence
        3. Remember "sale on approval" is bailment
    C. Abandoned property and adverse possession
        1. abandoned, giving possession with intent
        2. adverse (HELUVA)
            a. Hostile
            b. Exclusive
            c. Lasting (5 years)
            d. Uninterrupted
            e. Visible
            f. Actual
    D. Gifts
        1. Elements of Inter Vivos
            a. donative intent to pass title
            b. delivery
            c. acceptance (can be silence)
        2. Causa Mortis
            a. must be in contemplation of death
            b. If donor recovers, or donee dies first gift is revoked
        3. Special problems
            a. ring –guy
            b. mink – gal

II. Buyer Acquires Title of Seller
    A. Buyer may ACHIEVE title from seller (who never had title) in 7 cases
        1. Accession
        2. Cash
        3. Holder in due course
        4. Intermingling (common law confusion)
        5. Entrustment
            a. Owner

        b. Entrusts to merchant

        c. sells to buyer in ordinary course – buyer gets title

6. Voidable title
7. Estoppel – detrimental reliance, cloaking with incidia of ownership

Wills

I. Execution of wills

    A. Requirements for validly executed will

        1. Signed by testator (18) or proxy signature (at direction & in presence)

        2. two attesting witnesses

        3. each witness must sign in testator's presence

        4. Codicil must be executed with same formalities

        5. Exact order of signing is not critical as long as contemporaneous transaction

    B. Signing in testator's presence

        1. UPC/Majority Rule: T does not to actually see witnesses just be near enough that he is conscious of what they are doing

        2. IL Rule: Must be in interrupted scope of vision

    C. Attorney Liability for negligence in preparation of the will

        1. Minority Rule: no privity with others so only client can sue

        2. IL Rule: privity rejected as defense – intended beneficiaries can sue

    D. Interested witness Statute – beneficiary is attesting witness

        1. Will can be admitted to probate but beneficiary-witness loses legacy

            a. Unless two disinterested witnesses or would take either way

        2. executor not interested witness under majority rule (IL voids compensation)

        3. Under IL law signing by spouse of interested witness voids legacy too

        4. UPC states have abolished this rule

    E. Holographic wills

        1. UPC/Majority Rule: recognize handwritten and signed but unwitnessed wills

        2. IL Rule: do not recognize holographic wills because no witnesses

            a. foreign holographic wills can be admitted to probate

Model Answer: In about 30 states, including Michigan, the instrument would be valid as a holographic will because it was entirely in Testator's handwriting and signed by him. In Illinois, however, the instrument is not valid as will even though Testator may have intended it as such, because it was not witnessed by two witnesses.

    F. Conditional Wills

        1. court may interpret apparent condition to be motive for creating will

II. Revocation of Wills

    A. Valid Revocation – mere intent is not enough

        1. later testamentary instrument (appropriate formalities)

        2. physical act on the will itself

            a. Proof of Lost Wills Statute

                i. proof of due execution

                ii. cause of will's nonproduction

                iii. contents must be substantially proved

    B. Presumptions regarding revocation

        1. not found at death, last seen in testator's possession – presume revoked by physical act

        2. found mutilated at death, last seen in testator's possession – presume revoked by physical act

3. Neither of these applicable if last seen in someone else's possession

4. If more than one will: read together of possible – inconsistencies revoked by implication

C. Dependent Relative Revocation (DRR)

    1. IL no revival of revoked wills unless formalities observed

    2. DRR allows revocation to be set aside because of mistake of law or fact

D. Changes of face of will after it has been executed

    1. UPC/Majority Rule: change effective

    2. IL: ineffective to change will unless reexecuted with proper formalities

    3. Partial revocation by physical act is not valid

III. Beneficiary dies during testator's lifetime

  A. Anti-lapse statutes

    1. IL: applies only when the predeceasing beneficiary was a child or other descendant of the testator

    2. If anti-lapse does not apply, gift falls into residuary estate

  B. Lapse in residuary gift: "surviving residuary beneficiaries" rule

    1. IL: If the residuary estate is devised to two or more persons and gift to on of them lapses, the surviving residuary beneficiaries take the entire residuary estate, in proportion to their interest in the residue

    2. Anti-lapse statute trumps the "surviving residuary beneficiaries" rule if predeceasing beneficiary:

        a. was within the scope of the statute

        b. left descendants who survived the testator

  C. Class Gifts

    1. where class member predeceases testator, other member succeed to his share (look for anti-lapse if descendant)

    2. Rule of convenience – class closes when some member is entitled to distribution (gestation of 280 days for fetuses)

  D. Deaths in Quick Succession

    1. IL/Majority: Uniform Simultaneous Death Act: When title depends on order of deaths and there is no sufficient evidence that the person have died otherwise than simultaneously, the property of each passes as though he or she survived

        a. Wills: as though testator survived and beneficiary predeceased

        b. Intestacy: intestate survived and heir predeceased

        c. Insurance: though insured survived and beneficiary predeceased

    2. Several states have adopted 120-hr rule – need to live 120 hours to take

IV. Changes in Family after Will's Execution

    A. Testator Marries after will is executed

    1. UPC: testator write will then marries, the pretermitted spouse takes an intestate share of the estate

    2. IL (majority) – no effect on will (no omitted spouse rule)

        a. spouse protected by elective share

  B. Testator is divorced after will is executed

    1. IL (majority): Final decree of divorce or annulment revokes all gift and fiduciary appointments in favor of former spouse. Estate executed as if spouse predeceased the testator

  C. Testator has child after will executed – pretermitted child

1. IL (majority): Rule only applies to after born children (incl. republ.)
2. take as if no will (intestate) unless it appears from will omission intentional

V. Problems associated with testamentary gifts
   A. Abatement of Legacies – not enough assets to satisfy gifts and creditors attack gifts, order:
      1. intestate property
      2. residuary assets
      3. general legacies
      4. specific bequests
   B. Specifically bequeathed property not in estate at death – ademption
      1. gift fails if asset not there (blackacre)
      2. IL: if sales contract only partially performed devisee gets remaining
      3. If incapacity after bequest, devisee can sue for value if traceable
   C. Bequests of stocks and other securities
      1. generally seen as general legacies
      2. unless uses "my" then specific and ademption applies
      3. IL: includes everything but stock dividends
   D. Specific Gifts of Encumbered Property: Is lien "exonerated"
      1. common law/ majority: absent contrary provision, liens are exonerated from residuary estate
      2. IL/UPC: liens not exonerated – take as testator had

VI. Reference to Acts and events outside the will
   A. Incorporation by reference doctrine
      1. Extrinsic document, not present when the will was executed can be incorporated if:
         a. document in existence when will executed
         b. will must refer to document being in existence
         c. will describes sufficient to permit identification
      2. UPC exception - no disposition of money on tangible personal property
   B. Acts of independent significance (nontestamentary acts) – lifetime act with lifetime motive or purpose so even though it effects terms it is considered

VII. Other Will Doctrines
   A. Mistake or Ambiguity in the Will
      1. Plain meaning rule - extrinsic evidence inadmissible
      2. latent ambiguity because of misdescription – extrinsic evidence admissible (no declaration of intent)
         a. if evidence does not cure then gift fails
      3. patent ambiguity – mistake appears on face of will – extrinsic evidence admissible
   B. Contracts Relation to Wills (Joint or Mutual Wills)
      1. "Under the UPC and by statute in several states, a will is never contractual unless the will expressly states that a contract does exist. In Illinois and a number of states, however, execution of a joint will be a husband and wife may be found contractual IF all or mist if the following factors are present:
         a. will labeled joint and mutual
         b. will leaves entire estate to surviving spouse
         c. will disposes of all of their property in a unified disposition
         d. there is a common dispositive scheme on the death of the survivor

  2. If held contractual:
    a. apply will law
    b. apply contract law, breached will (constructive trust)
  3. Reciprocal wills are never presumed to be contractual unless clear and convincing evidence
 C. Effect of Words of Disheritance in a Will
  1. Under the UPC's negative bequest rule, a will can provide how property shall not be disposed of
  2. IL applies common law (majority), if will does not make complete disposition of estate, words of inheritance are ineffective (passes intestate)
 D. Unlawful conditions
  1. cannot induce divorce
  2. can make partial restraint on marriage
 E. Thou shalt not kill
  1. IL slayer statute: Killer forfeits interest in victim's estate if he intentionally and unjustifiably causes the death of another
  2. Applies to all forms of transfer
 F. Nonprobate assets
  1. property passing by rights of survivorship
  2. property passing by contract
  3. property held by revocable trust
VIII. Intestate Succession – (left no will, will denied probate, not complete disposition)
 A. Intestate Share of surviving spouse
  1. ½ if survived by descendants (family allowance regardless)
  2. all if not survived by descendants
 B. Inheritance by Descendants (Issue)
  1. strict per stirpes – one share for each line of living descendants
    a. descendants of deceased children take by representation
  2. cut at brother sister level if no kids
 C. Other intestate distribution rules
  1. Majority Rule: testator's estate inherited by parents if unmarried/no issues
  2. IL Rule: parents and siblings split shares
  3. parent disqualified if neglected, deserted, or failed to support child
 D. Adopted Children, Children Born out of Wedlock
  1. Children adopted under 18 have full inheritance
  2. unadopted stepchild cannot inherit
  3. adopted child has no inheritance from natural kin
  4. child adopted by spouse of natural parent has inheritance rights
  5. adopted over 18 inherits from parent only
  6. children born out of wedlock inherit from natural father if (PAP):
    a. Paternity suit
    b. Acknowledged paternity
    c. Probate proceedings
 E. Lifetime Gifts to Heir or Will Beneficiary
  1. common law: lifetime gift is presumed advancement of child's intestate share

2. IL (majority): reverses the common law presumption and requires writing: A lifetime gift is not advancement unless
    a. declared as such in writing by the donor
    b. acknowledged as such in writing by the donee
    c. applies only to children
3. non-children must be explicit
F. Disclaimer by heir or beneficiary
  1. Able to disclaim at any time in IL (whole or part)
  2. Treat as if predeceased
  3. Done to avoid gift tax and creditors claims

IX. Elective Share Statute – Right of Renunciation
  A. Amount of Elective Share
    1. 1/3 if survived by descendants
    2. ½ if not survived
  B. spouse must file notice of election to renounce will (IL 7 months)
  C. Election van be made by spouse or on incapacitated spouse's behalf
  D. All beneficiaries contribute pro rata – outright devises to spouse applied first
  E. Trusts
    1. UPC/Majority: Elective share applies to the augmented estate, which includes lifetime transfers in which the grantor retained the power to revoke, or to invade consume or dispose of principal
    2. IL: NO: Elective share means probate estate, does not apply to non-probate transfers

X. Will Contests – only those who have economic interest can contest
  A. Lack of Testamentary Capacity: Did testator have sufficient capacity to:
    1. understand the nature of the act he was doing
    2. know the nature and approximate value of his property
    3. know the natural objects of his bounty
    4. understand the disposition he was making
  B. undue Influence – contestants have burden to show:
    1. existence and exertion of undue influence
    2. effect of which has to overpower the mind and will of the testator
    3. product is a will that would not be created but for influence
    4. where a person is in a confidential or fiduciary relationship as active in procuring the will and that party will receive a substantial benefit under the will there is a presumption of undue influence which can be overcome with clear and convincing evidence
  C. No-contest clause
    1. lawful in IL even if probable cause
    2. lawful unless probable cause under UPC/majority

www.ingramcontent.com/pod-product-compliance
Lightning Source LLC
Chambersburg PA
CBHW080646180526
45168CB00008B/3322